D1528967

The New Era of Healthcare

Practical Strategies for Providers and Payers

Emad Rizk, MD

The New Era of Healthcare: Practical Strategies for Providers and Payers is published by HCPro, Inc.

Copyright © 2009 HCPro, Inc.

All rights reserved. Printed in the United States of America.   5   4   3   2   1

ISBN 978-1-60146-318-0

HCPro, Inc., provides information resources for the healthcare industry.

HCPro, Inc., is not affiliated in any way with The Joint Commission, which owns the JCAHO and Joint Commission trademarks.

Emad Rizk, MD, Author
Debra Beaulieu, Editor
Rick Johnson, Executive Editor
Matt Cann, Group Publisher
Susan Darbyshire, Art Director
Shane Katz, Cover Designer

Janell Lukac, Graphic Artist
Claire Cloutier, Copyeditor
Adam Carroll, Proofreader
Mattt Sharpe, Production Supervisor
Jean St. Pierre, Director of Operations

Advice given is general. Readers should consult professional counsel for specific legal, ethical, or clinical questions.

Arrangements can be made for quantity discounts. For more information, contact:

HCPro, Inc.
P.O. Box 1168
Marblehead, MA 01945
Telephone: 800/650-6787 or 781/639-1872
Fax: 781/639-2982
E-mail: *customerservice@hcpro.com*

Visit HCPro at its World Wide Web sites:
www.hcpro.com **and** ***www.hcmarketplace.com***

3/2009
21631

Contents

Contents

Acknowledgments

This book, which focuses principally on the power of collaboration, is in itself the product of a powerful collaboration. It draws on the wisdom of countless payer and hospital executives, physicians, nurses, and, of course patients, who have generously shared their concerns, ideas, and lessons learned with me over the years. In particular, I would like to thank:

My mother Isis, whose support, encouragement, and guidance I will be forever grateful.

My wife Fadia and my children, Antony, Michael, and Andrew, for understanding my endless travel and always being so supportive about the time it took to write this book.

Ricardo Guggenheim, MD, for his real-world insights and willingness to act as a sounding board for my ideas on a wide range of topics.

Bruce Jankowitz, Ross Homer, and Aria Marketing, for their counsel throughout the book development process.

Sandy Jacobs, whose outstanding writing expertise was invaluable to the creation of this book.

And to Christine Scarlett, for finding a way, as she always does, to make what seemed impossible possible.

About the Author

Emad Rizk, MD, is president of McKesson Health Solutions, a division of McKesson Corporation, delivering unique solutions that enable payers, providers, and patients to come together to transform the business and process of healthcare.

Rizk is a world-renowned expert in the healthcare industry, with more than 25 years of experience working with payers, physicians, hospital systems, and pharmaceutical organizations. He is a thought leader on transformational strategies and operational execution for healthcare organizations.

In his previous position as the global director of Deloitte, Rizk led medical cost and quality management practice across all industries. He also spearheaded the largest redesign of care management and delivery models among health plans and providers nationwide.

Rizk is sought after for his knowledge of the healthcare industry. He has served on many healthcare boards, including the National Clinical Advisory Board and National Quality Review, and currently serves on the boards of DMAA: Care Continuum Alliance, National Association for Hispanic Health, University of Miami, University of North Texas, and *Managed Care Magazine*. Rizk is a senior scholar professor at Jefferson Medical College in Philadelphia and has an extensive portfolio of published journal articles and books, including *The Wisdom of Top*

Health Care CEOs, a collection of interviews published in 2003 by the American College of Physician Executives.

In 2008, Rizk was named one of the "50 Most Powerful Physician Executives" in the United States by *Modern Physician* and one of the nation's top 25 leaders in disease management by *Managed Healthcare Executive.*

Rizk lives in Chicago with his wife Fadia and sons Antony, Michael, and Andrew.

Introduction

This is not an easy time for healthcare. Costs are up. Physician morale is down. Despite our growing medical knowledge, we seem unable to contain the burden of chronic disease. The cost, in dollars and human health, is astounding.

The most striking assessment of our healthcare system comes when we look abroad. The United States spends far more per capita on healthcare than any other country in the world. With that, we should have the world's top-rated healthcare, right? Unfortunately, we do not. While our costs have soared, our outcomes are not commensurate. Looking solely at mortality rates, many countries that spend a smaller portion of their gross domestic product on healthcare do significantly better.

So, it may surprise you that I am optimistic about the potential to improve the state of the U.S. healthcare system and the health of its patients. This improvement can be achieved through practical steps that focus largely on bringing together two critical constituents in healthcare: payers and providers.

For the past 20–30 years, payers and providers have been at odds with each other. Each move by insurers to control costs has been met with countermoves by hospitals and physicians to maintain their decision-making authority and payment levels. Our many strategies and models—from preferred health organizations, to health maintenance organizations to preferred provider organizations—have put payers and providers into every contorted relationship except as allies. No model yet has squarely addressed the critical relationship that must exist between payers and providers to ensure effective and cost-effective healthcare. The result is a system full of inefficiencies, redundancies, disconnects, and mistrust. These are some of the reasons that our healthcare system is in such distress.

But this dysfunction also opens a great window of opportunity. Payers and providers now have the incentive to put aside their old antagonisms. It is clear that the old ways of doing business cannot continue. Payers and providers face a shared challenge. Leaders on both sides are starting to see the fundamental need to work together toward mutual goals of healthcare efficiency and quality.

The term I use for this coming together is "alignment." My dictionary defines alignment as "the process of adjusting parts so that they are in proper relative position." Fortunately, we have the tools at hand to forge this alignment in the healthcare system. Payers and providers each have data that can drive better decisions and better care. Technologies exist that can bring all this data together. And each day brings new innovation—be it improved software to send real-time data from providers to payers, or a new device that enables a nurse to read biometric measures from a patient at home, miles away.

Will we have the motivation to master and use these technologies? Will we have the vision and road map to take the first steps?

In the pages that follow, I share my vision for healthcare. My goal is to help you look at your own region and your own sphere of influence differently and see the opportunities to bring about alignment. Whether you are a payer, provider, employer, or any other interested party, you can take steps toward a more efficient, productive health delivery system.

We need not wait for a master plan that will work for the entire country. I doubt such a thing exists. Experiments at the local level will show us what works and what does not, and will lead to models for the next round of experiments. This is how science moves forward. The same principle can apply in healthcare business innovation.

For the past 25 years, I have worked elbow-deep in the financial realities of healthcare and am intimately aware of the complexities. As a physician executive, I have experienced, implemented, and observed the many strategies and economic models that have come into play. I have stood at the juncture where interests meet (and sometimes compete) in healthcare—mostly between the payer and provider, but also between the employer and employee/consumer. I have seen what has worked and what has not. And I am certain that every model tried so far has been less than optimal because it failed to address the critical relationship that must exist between the payer and provider.

I embarked on writing this book to share the big picture from where I sit. My strategies for alignment present practical ideas to change the way that payers and providers interact. These strategies create a means to improve quality and manage costs. I hope you will recognize ways in which you can apply some of these ideas to your own challenges.

As a physician and an executive, I see how healthcare is at the center of our future prosperity. Personal health is key to maintaining productivity for each individual. And for companies throughout our economy, healthcare expenditures go right to the bottom line. How we fix healthcare is critical to so much of the economic health of our country, and our global competitiveness.

Any solution must create a situation in which all parties benefit. Alignment is critical. I invite you to join in building a new paradigm for the payer-provider relationship. If we combine forces, we can take on and successfully solve the issues plaguing healthcare.

Chapter 1
Why Payers and Providers Are Disconnected

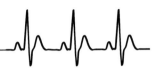

Two major stakeholders—the providers of healthcare and the entities that pay for it—affect the cost, quality, and outcome of healthcare delivery in the United States today. Yet, for nearly three decades, these two groups have been at odds. As healthcare and the way we pay for it have evolved, each group has adopted tactics to manage costs and leverage its own assets in ways that seemed reasonable. But the tactics of each group have increasingly alienated the other and widened the gulf of mistrust.

Over these same decades, we have witnessed great progress in diagnosing and treating disease, for which the medical community can be justifiably proud. On the payer side, insurers have innovated new products and technologies that help to manage the costs associated with the rapid expansion of medical technologies. However, we find ourselves with a healthcare system that costs more than ever, delivers less quality and efficiency than we would like, and lags behind most other developed countries in key indicators and cost. Therefore, it is time to refocus the energies of payers and providers on working together toward collaborative accountability.

Understanding the Disconnect

To understand the disconnect, let's look at how it evolved. Private health insurance and employer-sponsored healthcare emerged in the 1930s and 1940s, and put in place a fee-for-service model that dominated for 40 years. Under this indemnity system, patients paid all costs out of pocket up to a deductible (typically $2,000) and then a percentage (typically 2%) of all subsequent costs. Increasingly, technological and expensive care led to the rise of managed care, in which employers, insurers, and medical providers sought to contain costs, improve performance, and increase coordination of services.[1] We have seen an evolution in managed care from health maintenance organizations to preferred provider organizations to point-of-service plans and, most recently, to consumer-directed products.

Managed care—defined as any system that manages care with the aim of controlling costs while satisfying medical quality standards—should have brought about an alignment among employers, insurers, and providers. But because payers and providers did not cooperate to find solutions, that did not happen. Instead, each party was looking after its own interests rather than exploring ways to work together.

With each new iteration of managed care, payers developed new tactics to control costs, some more successful than others. Payers instituted tools that either managed or controlled access to care. Through contracting, fees for some services were reduced. Capitation, a fixed payment to care for patients regardless of how intense their medical needs may be, shifted the financial risk to the provider. The gatekeeper role of the primary care physician (PCP), ostensibly to ensure appropriate use of specialists, quickly took on a negative connotation to patients and physicians who perceived the PCP as limiting access to care.

Meanwhile, hospitals were penalized with denials—for example, if a patient was readmitted within several days of discharge. Such penalties were intended to deliver more value by making hospitals and providers more efficient and effective. However, because most hospitals did not have the appropriate processes in place to improve care, the payers' actions were perceived as squeezing providers. And although hospitals and providers have become significantly more efficient, these changes have not led to the results we need to transform healthcare.

What nearly all of these tactics have in common—perhaps with the exception of the emerging consumer-directed movement—is that they are not aligned with provider incentives. Providers have responded with strategies of their own. Individual hospitals consolidated into hospital systems and sole practitioners into physician groups. Although many factors drove this process, one clear impetus was to increase the bargaining power of providers with payers. Providers, especially hospitals, applied rigorous review to their contracts. Contract negotiation became ever more arduous, often with nine months spent bargaining for a 12-month contract. With the advent of new technologies, providers drove innovation in tools to improve the billing cycle. In essence, providers, primarily hospitals, became fixated on revenue optimization when they could have focused on delivering more value to patients and becoming more efficient.

The lack of alignment between providers and payers has led to distorted behaviors. Managed care plans, when seeking to trim their expenses, tend to look at line items that cost a lot of money, particularly high-volume procedures such as cataract and cardiac procedures, and reflexively lower physician reimbursement. In response, many providers attempt to maintain their income by increasing the volume of procedures they perform.

Physicians can increase volume in two ways. First, they can expand their patient base, which is not a feasible option for most. The second is to increase the number of procedures performed within the same patient pool by adopting more liberal decision-making. Consider the example of cataract surgery. Although there are clear guidelines recommending when a cataract should be removed, significant latitude and judgment can be applied when cataract disease is evident and the patient's vision is at stake without intervention. Therefore, some ophthalmologists looking to increase their procedure volume may become more aggressive in their treatment.

Managed care's most recent attempts to manage costs have come in the form of cost and quality rankings of physicians and hospitals. Plans use rankings within their markets to create tiers of physicians based on cost and quality data, and then use financial penalties on lower-tier performers. For example, plans charge consumers higher copayments for lower-tiered physicians. No managed care tactic has elicited a stronger organized response from physicians, who have not largely been consulted about how rankings were devised or imposed. More mistrustful of managed care than ever, physicians have rallied against these new programs. In Massachusetts, for example, the state medical society sued the state's Group Health Insurance Commission, charging that lower-ranked doctors were defamed and consumers who paid more for lower-tier physicians were defrauded.[2]

A Changing Universe for Physicians

Delivery of care ultimately is managed directly by providers. This is true no matter what program or practice standard is put in place and no matter what name it is given. The physician orders the tests, decides whether to admit a patient, and recommends one course of treatment over another. It is the physician who ultimately has the greatest influence over the quality of care, and, less directly, its cost.

To understand the environment of managed care—and to make any important changes—we need to take into account how the ground has shifted for physicians as a profession.

The past few decades have seen enormous disruption to physicians. The average income for a physician in the United States, adjusted for inflation, dropped by 7.1% from 1995 to 2003.[3] PCPs saw their inflation-adjusted income drop the most—10.2% on average—while the income of surgical specialists dropped 8.2% and that of medical specialists fell 2.1%. Meanwhile, during the same period, salaries for other professional and technical workers increased by 6.9%.[4]

While their own income was slipping, physicians were acutely aware of a rising class of hospital and health plan administrators and executives with salaries exceeding their own. Perhaps more than the salaries, physicians were bothered by what they perceived as the emergence of medical managers who threatened to eclipse physician autonomy in decision-making.

Throughout the 1980s, the principles of industrial engineering were newly applied to many businesses, including healthcare. It was evident that the concept of "total quality management" and other approaches to improving quality and efficiency could be very useful in healthcare settings. But as administrators imposed these policies, physicians felt their toes were being stepped on. Part of the change was the rise in clinical guidelines, which first emerged from specialty physician groups. Increasingly, these guidelines—soon to be known as evidence-based medicine (EBM)—became part of managed care organizations' requirements. Although there is now universal embrace of EBM as a hallmark for quality (as I'll explain in the next chapter), the early move toward clinical practice guidelines was viewed by some physicians as "cookbook medicine" that usurped their judgment and experience.

This new attention to efficiency occurred because medical care had become episodic, in a way that was not best for the patient, the provider, or the payer. For example, a patient might see a new doctor about chronic headaches. And the workup might lead to an expensive MRI, an important test to eventually rule out a brain tumor. But if that physician had a record of the patient's history showing a prior condition that could be contributing to the headache or that the patient had repeatedly visited other physicians with complaint of headache and perhaps already had an MRI, the physician might have taken a more effective—and less expensive—course of action.

There are many reasons we have reached this degree of episodic care: changes in reimbursement practices in the past 30 years, the rise of specialists, and simply the way doctors are trained to think and practice. This trend toward episodic care has had all sorts of implications for the cost and quality of care. It also has made the practice of medicine less satisfying for physicians, who have lost the personal connection to patients that typically develops over time and across multiple medical issues. The challenge now is to bring back continuity of care for physicians and their patients.

A physician's career satisfaction is difficult to measure over time and varies by specialty and setting. But according to a study of physicians from 1997 to 2001, the factors most strongly associated with satisfaction levels were threats to physician autonomy, physicians' ability to manage day-to-day patient interactions and time, and their ability to provide high-quality care. Declining income was not as strongly associated with changes in satisfaction.[5]

If physicians were not already feeling under siege, the past decade has brought a spate of much-publicized reports regarding medical errors, patient safety, and physician misjudgment. A well-known report from the Institute of Medicine in

1999 suggested that as many as 44,000–98,000 people die in hospitals each year as a result of medical errors and that medical errors cost $37.6 billion annually, with approximately $17 billion of these costs associated with preventable errors (about half of which are for direct healthcare costs rather than administration).[6]

More recently, we've seen reports of physician decision-making that resulted in underuse and overuse of medical services. In 2006, the RAND Corporation looked at the 30 acute and chronic conditions that constitute leading causes of death and disability and found that patients received about 55% of recommended care.[7] In the same year, another study reported that overuse of three diagnostic tests during routine health exams—urinalysis, x-rays, and electrocardiograms— cost between $47 million and $194 million annually.[8]

Among many efforts to rein in costs of preventable errors and mistreatment, the government initiated a program to penalize providers for poor care. Hospitals, in particular, are feeling the squeeze from this initiative. In 2007, Medicare instituted a policy of not reimbursing for preventable medical problems among patients who already were hospitalized.[9] Private insurers are beginning to follow suit and have adopted similar measures.

For physicians, changing employment trends reflect—and in some areas are driving—the working life of physicians. In coming years, we expect an increasing number of physicians to be employed by a hospital system; by some estimates, it may be up to 60%. The percentage of female physicians rose from 11.6% in 1980 to 26.6% in 2004.[10] By 2006, women made up more than 48% of medical school graduates.[11] The desire to balance work and family has led an increasing number of physicians, both male and female, to seek more predictable work hours than their demanding profession has traditionally required. More physicians are also seeking part-time work. A recent study showed that four out of 10 pediatric residents seek part-time employment after graduation and two out of 10 find and accept part-time jobs.[12]

Those of us in the business of bringing technology to physicians also see a generation gap between more seasoned physicians and their younger peers. The physician leadership, who make decisions on behalf of their profession, may not be in sync with their younger colleagues, who generally are more fluent users of the newer technologies of connectivity. Younger physicians as a group adopt new technologies easily and fully expect to use such technologies to diminish their administrative burdens, whereas some seasoned physicians remain skeptical or unmotivated to embrace technology. Despite the difficulties posed by the generation gap, healthcare leaders have an opportunity to work with physicians who are early adopters of technology to drive new efficiencies and collaboration.

Traditionally, the managed care industry's behavior toward physicians has been based on the incorrect assumption that providers are motivated primarily by financial incentives. This fallacy is one reason why so many attempts to manage care have not met their hoped-for results—and instead have fueled the cycle of mistrust. No doubt that finances matter, but there is much more to physician behavior than just money.

True alignment with physicians requires understanding the realities of their work life—their frustrations, their expectations, and their aspirations. The truth is that physicians feel great responsibility toward their patients, and are motivated primarily by the desire to do what is medically best for those under their care. So there is an enormous opportunity to focus on what is truly a shared goal: keeping patients healthy and restoring them to health when they fall ill.

Physicians also like efficiency, at least in concept, and solving problems. Reaching out to physicians and engaging them on a nonfinancial level is essential. I will address this further in Chapter 2 and throughout this book.

Many Players on One Stage

We cannot consider the payer-provider relationship without touching upon the other constituencies and trends that influence our healthcare system. These include:

- **Employers.** Employers are the drivers of health insurance, with increasing involvement in controlling costs and maintaining a healthy population. Large employers and business consortiums such as the National Business Group on Health have driven much of the innovation we've seen in recent years.

- **Patients.** The consumer health movement that began in the late 1960s, with patients playing a larger role in healthcare decision-making, has exploded in the last decade with the availability of health information on the Web. In a twist on patient empowerment, one of the most recent cost-control measures by insurers and employers has been consumer-directed products that shift costs to consumers. The intent of these plans is to motivate patients to seek out the most cost-efficient and high-quality care. But do consumers have the right information to make these decisions? And how do individual patients balance questions of cost and quality? Whether consumer-directed programs truly manage care has yet to be proven.

- **Government.** Government is a huge player, accounting for half of all healthcare spending in the United States, and creating policies that affect all payers. But it is the private sector that will drive the innovation needed now.

- **New health challenges.** Although a subset of the population may be in better health than ever, other health challenges have emerged—particularly in the areas of obesity, diabetes, asthma, and HIV. Most far-reaching of these challenges, perhaps, is the increasing number of patients without insurance or with inadequate insurance. These patients increasingly turn to hospitals for primary care, and hospitals must absorb the financial burden.

Entire books could be written about each of these factors in the healthcare system. However, this book will focus on the relationship between payers and providers—and how improving that relationship will bring benefits to all.

Where Do We Turn Next?

Continuing "business as usual" is not an option. Among those involved in healthcare, there increasingly is talk that the system as we know it cannot continue. Everywhere you look, there are dour assessments of the state of healthcare in the United States: discouraging measures of health outcomes dropping amid the highest healthcare costs in the world, painfully slow adoption of new technology, and a high percentage of the population without adequate primary care. And we are right to sound the alarm about healthcare as an industry. From 2006 to 2008, the medical loss ratio (the percentage of a health plan's revenue used to pay for medical services) for large public plans rose from 81.7% to 83.7%. This drove an erosion of market value for those plans by $70 billion in just the first half of 2008.

As an industry, we have shifted costs in every direction we can. We have done everything possible—except initiate the kind of changes that will get to the heart of the problems and create long-term benefits. It is time to stop shifting costs and instead align payers and providers around their common goals. Now is the time to bring together the two major constituents that affect cost, quality, and outcomes. Payers and providers must collaborate in a meaningful way to truly manage the care and costs for our patients. And it all comes down to the need for alignment in three basic areas: clinical, economic, and administrative.

ENDNOTES

1. V. Rodwin, "The Rise of Managed Care in the United States: Lessons for French Health Policy," published with permission at *www.nyu.edu/projects/rodwin/managedcare.html* (accessed December 5, 2008) from C. Altenstetter and J. Bjorkman (editors), *Health Policy Reform, National Schemes and Globalization* (London: Macmillan; New York: St. Martin's Press, 1997).

2. J. Krasner, "Physician Group Files Suit over Rankings," *The Boston Globe,* May 22, 2008, *www.boston.com/business/healthcare/articles/2008/05/22/physicians_group_files_suit_over_rankings* (accessed December 5, 2008).

3. Ha T. Tu and Paul B. Ginsburg, "Losing Ground: Physician Income, 1995–2003, Tracking Report No. 15, June 2006, Table 1," Center for Studying Health System Change *Community Tracking Study Physician Survey, www.hschange.com/CONTENT/851/851.pdf* (accessed October 3, 2008).

4. Ha T. Tu and Paul B. Ginsburg, "Losing Ground: Physician Income, 1995–2003, Tracking Report No. 15, June 2006, Table 1," Center for Studying Health System Change *Community Tracking Study Physician Survey, www.hschange.com/CONTENT/851/851.pdf* (accessed October 3, 2008).

5. B.E. Landon, J. Reschovsky, and D. Blumenthal, "Changes in Career Satisfaction Among Primary Care and Specialist Physicians, 1997–2001," *Journal of the American Medical Association* 289 (4): 442–449.

6. L. Kohn, J. Corrigan, and M. Donaldson (editors), *To Err Is Human: Building a Safer Health System, The Institute of Medicine,* Committee on the Quality of Healthcare in America (Washington, DC: National Academy Press, 2000), as summarized at *www.ahrq.gov/qual/errback.htm.*

7. S. Asch, E. Kerr, J. Keesey, J. Adams, C. Setodji, S. Malik, and E. McGlynn, "Who Is at Greatest Risk for Receiving Poor-Quality Health Care?" *New England Journal of Medicine,* 354:(2006)1147–1156.

8. D. Merenstein, G. Daumit, and N. Powe, "Use and Costs of Nonrecommended Tests During Routine Preventive Health Exams," *American Journal of Preventive Medicine* 30(6): 521–527 D.

9. *http://blogs.wsj.com/health/2008/08/01/medicare-expands-list-of-no-pay-hospital-conditions* (accessed December 5, 2008).

10. Derek R. Smart, *Characteristics and Distribution in the U.S,* 2006 Edition (American Medical Association Press, 2006), 4.

11. Association of Medical Colleges, "AAMC: FACTS Table 29: Women Enrollment and Graduates in U.S. Medical Schools 1961–2006," AAMC Data Warehouse: Student section; Student Records System (SRS*); Journal of Medical Education, www.aamc.org/data/facts/2007/women-count.htm* (accessed October 3, 2008).

12. William L. Cull, et al., "Many Pediatric Residents Seek and Obtain Part-time Positions," *Pediatrics* 121, 2 (February, 2008): 276–281.

Chapter 2

What Is Needed: Three Types
of Alignment

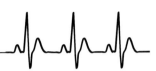

The fundamental need in today's healthcare system is for the two largest constituents payers and providers—to work together in alignment. We need a change in thinking and actions to shift the dynamic of how payers and providers work and interact with each other.

From the payer's point of view, most costs—85%—are devoted to patient care and the administration that goes with it. My vision is to break the endless cycle of push-and-pull around those costs and to finally align payers and providers toward their common goals. This proposal is not altruistic, but practical. After decades of shifting the economic burden and risk, it makes sense for payers to align themselves with those who control 85% of costs. For providers, it makes sense to accept responsibility for the health and well-being of the patients they care for and share the risks and rewards of good outcomes. And, for everyone involved, reducing bureaucracy and inefficiency makes sense.

It is easy to get overwhelmed by the magnitude of the problems we face in healthcare. But it is possible to break down the problems into smaller pieces, on which we can take action. I believe there are three key areas in which payers and providers must align:

- **Clinical.** Identify the best treatments from evidence-based medicine (EBM) and mutually determine appropriate care.

- **Economic.** Agree on costs in advance, in detail and with full transparency.

- **Administrative.** Create and use tools to diminish the administrative burden for all parties and increase efficiency.

Granted, these are three large areas, but a lot can be done with each through a commitment to collaboration and business alignment. By alignment, I mean that payers and providers should agree on clearly defined goals in patient care, how costs will be paid, and what tools will be available to help reach those goals. This means bringing together resources, rather than using them to work around or against each other.

How Alignment Will Work

Health plans and providers need each other. Payers have vast amounts of historical claims data, while providers have the clinical data. These are two very different kinds of information, both referring to the same patients. Combining the two could be powerful. Neither payers nor providers are there yet. Yes, both parties talk about collaborating and sharing information with each other, but neither is truly doing it. In fact, both groups use much of this information to check up on the other. So we are missing the opportunity to drive up efficiency and deliver better care to patients because of a lack of alignment and collaboration. It is time to move forward on this vast opportunity to bring this information together and use it to better our industry.

A key ingredient that is desperately missing to connect the care process between payers and providers is trust. Payers and providers just don't trust each other. A first step toward trust is for payers and providers to agree, up front, what information they will share. And they must agree to share that data in a transparent way. Transparency will engender trust.

Transparency is a popular buzzword right now, applied to many industries and relationships. But it truly describes what is necessary to align payers and providers in a fruitful manner. For our purposes, transparency means that each constituency shares data that could be useful to the other. This means that payers make fully available and understandable to providers all the rules that govern what they are paid. This enables providers—both hospitals and physicians—to understand how their reimbursement is determined and what factors influence the payments they receive. This knowledge will become ever more crucial as providers are increasingly reimbursed for outcomes rather than for the interventions they deliver. Meanwhile, payers would fully learn from providers the clinical outcomes they are—or are not—achieving. This exchange would help to compensate providers appropriately and also enable payers to help identify patients who would benefit from greater efforts to reach them.

But this collaborative approach goes further, in ways that can help both payer and provider in a sort of feedback loop and, ultimately, benefit the patient, too. For example, let's say that, in this model, a physician is expected to identify all patients with a certain condition and put them on a care plan. The physician also would make available to the payer all clinical data relating to these patients. The payer would provide analytic support, using prescription and other data, to guide the physician toward patients who are most in need of attention so that their care can be prioritized. Ultimately, the physician gets paid to identify disease early, the payer truly optimizes its efforts toward managing the medical risk in its portfolio, and patients get better-quality, more cost-efficient care. The linchpin is the shared data—which ideally is stored in a common database that both groups could access. The payer and provider would be working toward a shared outcome. Along with sharing information, this model would enable payers and providers to share economic rewards.

The shared goal of payers and providers is to connect the care process, the economics that pay for and reward good care, and the administrative framework that makes it all happen. That is a broad-brush view of alignment. Now, let's break it down into the three key areas I mentioned earlier in this chapter.

1. Clinical alignment

Today, we are fortunate to have at our disposal abundant EBM data that payers and providers can use to help implement clinical alignment. This success can then be used to achieve alignment where evidence is not readily available, but standards of medical care are.

It may be hard to believe that, as recently as the early 1970s, when the popular show *Marcus Welby, MD,* was on television, what we then called "modern medicine" in fact lacked hard evidence for many common practices. The acknowledgment that medical practice relied on experience and judgment, but not clear data, led to the increased development of EBM in the early 1970s.

Since then, researchers have conducted increasing numbers of randomized controlled studies to compare one therapeutic option with another or to measure the result of a specific therapy. EBM uses the data and analysis from these well-designed studies and applies the lessons learned to the decision-making for individual patients. Combined with a clear understanding of the patient's circumstances and good clinical judgment, EBM has had a powerful effect on patient outcomes and has been a critical component in setting standards for medical care.

Given that it's always easier to align people around evidence than opinions, you would expect that EBM would have been immediately and universally embraced. However, as used in a managed care setting, EBM initially created some waves and was sometimes misunderstood. Physicians often felt that payers overly relied on EBM to justify denying treatment outside the guidelines, when some individual patients in fact warranted a different, more customized approach. On the other hand, payers sometimes felt that doctors were resistant to change.

Indeed, EBM has limitations. Study results are not always as straightforward as we might like—due to study design, the way researchers frame a question, and the complexities of disease processes. Adoption of EBM has been slow because not all physicians keep up with new medical findings. Also, some are skeptical about changing course from what they have been doing for patients for decades. For example, although it has long been clear from the evidence that beta-blockers greatly benefit patients with heart failure, it was decades before they were widely adopted.

By now, it is universally acknowledged that EBM offers the most effective guide to patient care, especially when used in concert with the judgment of an experienced physician and with flexibility allowed for the customs and standards of the community. Clinical guidelines used by payers generally combine EBM data with the consensus from experts on how a particular problem is best treated. Today, EBM is the cornerstone of medical practice—and it should also be the cornerstone of clinical alignment between payers and providers.

A good example of clinical alignment, as I envision it, could be seen in the Chapter 1 example of determining when a cataract should be removed. Clinical alignment would call for providers and payers to agree—based on evidence—when a cataract should be removed. Because removal of a cataract is based on both objective (a vision test) and subjective (effect on a patient's life) measures, a shared guideline would take both factors into account.

Now, let's examine coronary artery angioplasty for a blockage. What does the evidence say is the appropriate time to perform angioplasty? When a coronary artery is 60% occluded? 70%? The evidence may show that, in most patients, angioplasty should be used when a specific artery is blocked by more than 70%.

In both of the above examples, a clinician and a payer would have a predetermined guideline that is easily accessible and would describe—based on evidence—the most appropriate course of action. But the use of evidence-based guidelines within a managed care environment is not intended to hamstring a physician. For example, after a heart attack, it would be expected that all patients would be prescribed a beta-blocker. But a physician may run into circumstances in which beta-blockers may be contraindicated because of conditions such as severe lung disease, in which case a different course of action would be necessary.

These are examples of how payers and providers might align around treatment for a specific procedure. But I also have in mind a much more basic clinical alignment: a simple, shared goal between payer and provider to make sure the most fundamental screenings and care reach patients with chronic disease.

We know that the top five chronic diseases—diabetes, congestive heart failure, hypertension/coronary artery disease, chronic obstructive pulmonary disease, and asthma—account for 50% percent of all healthcare costs. But we also know that only a small percentage of those with chronic disease are diagnosed. And of those who are diagnosed with these conditions, many are not well-controlled because of inadequate care or poor patient compliance. Clinical alignment also means a shared commitment by the payer and provider to reach and engage people who are not receiving adequate care to control their disease.

For example, take diabetes care. The payer and provider might agree on the following three goals for diabetes care:

- The provider must identify all diabetes patients in his or her practice

- All identified patients must receive a care plan

- All diabetes patients must regularly receive the basic tests (hemoglobin A1c, a retinal exam, and kidney function test) to monitor their level of disease control

This is clinical alignment, with the goal of early identification and treatment of a chronic disease. The benefits come down the road, from saving the considerable costs incurred by an emergency such as diabetic coma or loss of vision.

Providing the right care, at the right time, in the right setting, has been a mantra in healthcare in recent years. Clinical alignment is the way to do it. This clinical alignment toward continuous, rather than episodic, care is good for the payer and good for the patient. But it requires buy-in from the provider, especially the physician, who needs appropriate compensation and support. This is where economic and administrative alignment play a role.

2. Economic alignment

The simplest and most obvious form of economic alignment is for payers and providers to agree on the cost of services—in advance and in detail, through the contracting process. This requires that contracts be transparent and easy to understand. Tools already exist to automate the contracting process. We know that contract automation reduces negotiation time, streamlines changes, eliminates errors, and enables further automation such as auto-adjudication. These elements are essential to reducing the time spent on denials and appeals, which is an important underpinning of economic alignment.

But economic alignment should go beyond agreement on costs. True economic alignment begins when the physician, the hospital, and the health plan align around a specific outcome. They must agree what providers will be paid for achieving that outcome, and all parties must feel there is equity in the alignment.

One very simple form of economic alignment could be that the plan and the physicians agree that the physicians will receive preset payment for each diabetes patient and will be free to use those dollars as they see fit.

The most obvious and widespread form of economic or financial alignment is pay for performance (P4P). The challenge is to keep the measures simple, yet aligned with outcomes. Thinking back to the example of clinical goals for patients with diabetes, we can see how a three-tiered P4P plan could work. A physician's first payment would come simply for identifying a patient with diabetes and populating a database with that patient's demographic and clinical information. A second payment would be triggered when the patient is put on a care plan agreed to by both physician and payer. A third payment would come when that patient undergoes tests for hemoglobin A1c, retinal health, and kidney function, and the results are entered in the database.

One problem with P4P, as it has been used in recent years, has been its narrow focus on rewarding specific actions, rather than contributing to improving the continuum of care. For a plan to pay incentives for a particular, limited action may actually misalign care. It is human nature to chase an incentive. A physician who is paid specifically to look at the hemoglobin A1c test may focus on completing that objective, without looking at the bigger picture of care for his or her diabetes patients, and may exclude other important diagnostic indicators and treatments that do not have incentives attached.

Financial incentives to physicians evolved by identifying aspects of care that a payer could measure through a claim, which made it possible for the process to be industrialized. We must ensure that, in the future, the economic reward structure is focused more globally on outcomes. Economic alignment occurs when payment helps lead to desired outcomes. For example, a more expansive way to address economic alignment is to create P4P—or pay-for-participation—mechanisms that reward outcomes in sync with the optimal results found in evidence-based guidelines.

Again, trust is crucial. Without trust, providers may be concerned that payers are simply trying another tactic to pay less or shift risk to them. And payers will be wary that providers will work toward the financial rewards rather than the overall objectives and desired outcomes.

This is why shared accountability—I call it collaborative accountability—must be built into the relationship between payers and providers. Both payers and providers are accountable for addressing the chronic diseases that make up the majority of our healthcare spending. (Patients, of course, are accountable for following their care plans.) But it is payers who must step up to provide and pay for the tools of alignment. This commitment from payers will engender the trust of physicians.

Health plans are in a position to provide the infrastructure and technology that bring together financial and clinical information. Plans already are the repository of much of our healthcare data: claims data, laboratory values, benefit and eligibility information, and more. Paying for the technology to make this information accessible to physicians at the point of care would help physicians move from episodic care to delivering care focused on the continuum. To play their part within this collaborative accountability, physicians must commit to using these tools. For economic alignment to be achieved, providers' responsibilities must be articulated clearly, the outcomes must be measurable, and providers must be adequately compensated.

3. Administrative alignment

Although economic alignment is usually seen as the primary incentive to physicians, health plans have an equally effective tool in their arsenal: They can relieve the administrative burden on the provider. Think of all the staff needed to support a single practicing physician: a nurse, a receptionist, someone to handle authorizations and billing. According to some estimates, physicians spend 15%–20% of their time on administrative tasks—time that could be spent one-on-one with patients. Technology offers many solutions to achieve greater efficiency in the delivery of healthcare, if we choose to invest in and use it.

Looking ahead, we anticipate that a greater percentage of the physician work force will be employed by hospitals. Many physicians are now seeking a work environment in which they are not responsible for the details of running a small business, as self-employed physicians have been. One way to provide the quality of life these physicians want is to diminish the time they spend on administrative chores. Relieving the administrative burden of a practice can be a very powerful incentive for these physicians.

Plans can align with providers by offering administrative ease. For physicians, electronic medical records, e-prescribing tools, and electronic access to clinical guidelines automate administrative functions and contribute to effectiveness and efficiency. These tools connect the physician to the payer in a way that the physician values. At the front desk and in the back office, payers can help provide tools that enable staff to submit claims electronically rather than manually and to check what is authorized at the point of care. The aim of administrative alignment is to break the cycle of denials and appeals that is so time-consuming and costly. If we can remove just 10%–20% of the inefficiency and paperwork that is generated in the back-and-forth between providers and payers, administrative costs will drop, and physicians will have more time for patient care.

Administrative alignment can involve patient history data that helps the physician make better decisions and can be leveraged across an entire care team to more efficiently deliver better care.

Collaboration between payers and providers is necessary so that physicians help determine what types of administrative support would be most helpful for reaching clinical goals. If a payer has identified high emergency room use by asthma patients in a practice, that payer might ask whether a 24-hour 1-800 hotline to a nurse might help. The alignment comes when a payer funds the hotline and then finds that emergency room visits drop.

Alignment around administration brings together the clinical and financial relationships between provider and payer—and has the potential to reduce costs for both parties. Creating the administrative tools is a wise investment for the payer, both in building efficiency and in cultivating goodwill with the provider.

Although we will explore alignment in much greater detail in later chapters, the basic scenario is this: The provider commits to identifying patients in need, follows an agreed-upon care plan, and provides all relevant clinical data to the payer. In return, the payer provides analytical support to help guide the physician, support aid in clinical care (a care team approach for medical care), and provide administrative relief to mitigate costs and improve efficiency. The compensation is agreed upon in advance and regarded as equitable.

The financial model for alignment is both powerful and simple. Providers will focus their energies on patients presenting the greatest opportunity to affect costs, particularly future costs, in the form of catastrophic events. Payers will channel their investigative capabilities (analytics) to help providers find the patients with the greatest need and, therefore, financial exposure. Alignment will also reduce costs for low-value administrative activities that cannibalize patient care time and drive up the cost of care.

Without alignment, we cannot get rid of waste and inefficiency. Without alignment, we cannot seize upon the enormous potential of information-sharing technology. Without alignment, we cannot reward and perpetuate good practices.

But with alignment, we can bring high-quality and cost-effective care to our patients. In Chapter 3, I will explain how to begin defining and creating a pilot program to harness the power of alignment.

Chapter 3

Getting Started: Creating a Pilot Project

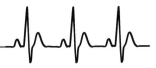

When we think about change in healthcare, we should look to bring change to one geographic region at a time. Each region has its own practice patterns, insurers, government structures, and population characteristics. Within a single region, we have the greatest opportunity to learn what works and what does not, and how to achieve alignment and success. In this chapter, I will explain how to choose an area for a pilot and how to construct a meaningful pilot. When a successful pilot is executed in a single region, lessons can be learned that are meaningful for the industry and that can be deployed on a larger scale.

I've always believed that healthcare changes are more likely to occur on a regional basis than through any overarching national policy change. Widespread policy changes too often have the feel of forcing a square peg into a round hole. If you try long and hard enough, you may wear down the edges of the square into some semblance of a round hole—but not without a lot of damage. The federal government, of course, has access to the massive appropriations that can be used to initiate change and is free of the constraints of Wall Street. These conditions are what made it possible for the government to initiate Medicare and Medicaid. But in more recent times, we've seen that it is not politically achievable for our national government to drive the innovations that can bring about the alignments within healthcare that are so desperately needed.

Looking at our large nation, I see a need to understand the differences within our diverse populace. Whether it's variations in population or practice patterns or business models, we need to accept that one size does not fit all. The differences among us may be as important—and as necessary to understand—as the commonalities we've focused on so far.

But who is in a position to truly bring about change? I believe the payers, more than any other constituency, are in the best position. Payers have the magnitude and the capabilities. Payers have the means to invest in the change. And, to some degree, payers have already gained much experience with the technologies that will drive positive change.

But private insurers cannot do it alone. They need the participation and support of hospital systems, physicians, and state or regional governments to be successful. These groups can also spearhead change. They too will need support to succeed.

A state or local government can form a strong and effective partnership with a local health system or regional payer. Even large states, with Medicaid budgets in excess of $20–$30 billion, can work toward the kind of changes I have in mind. They can do so by focusing on a particular population or a particular problem within the state. And, although payers have initiated most of the pilot programs I know of, I am seeing more hospital systems leading the process of aligning with payers for the benefit of all. I am encouraged to see multiple stakeholders bringing solutions forward for managing costs while achieving high-quality care.

In the rest of this chapter, we will explore ways to experiment with alignment in your own region. As you think about creating your own pilot project, bear in mind these watchwords: transparency, simplicity, narrow focus, and line-of-sight approach.

Drive with Your Eyes Open

"Drive with your eyes wide open," I like to say. By this, I mean that it is important to gather as much relevant information as possible and do a thorough analysis. This is especially true as you set out to define a pilot project. In nearly every market and every population, we know that if we could intervene early in the most prevalent chronic diseases, we could keep people healthier for longer and save costs downstream. Any pilot program to improve the well-being and healthcare costs for a population will likely focus on one of the big five chronic diseases: diabetes, congestive heart failure (CHF), hypertension and coronary artery disease, chronic obstructive pulmonary disease, or asthma.

As we learn more about the role of mental health and its relationship to physical health, depression also may join this list of high-impact diseases.

The overarching goal is to learn which tactics can preserve health and avoid the calamitous events that lead to high costs and disabling disease. The true leaders among us will think beyond their own constituency—be it hospital, doctor, or payer—and figure out how all these groups can work together to bring about change.

The first step is to define a geographic region that you already know fairly well and that is well-contained. A pilot project need not focus on the most representative population within your market. Rather, it should involve a population and an area—be it a state, county, or region—that is well-suited to be the subject of the experiment. The key factor is to have a concentration of payers, providers, and patients. Aspects to be considered include regional population concentration, the physician pool, the hospital(s) involved, and disease patterns in the region. The more contained an area, the better. Let's examine these factors in greater detail.

Population and disease density

Strive to understand, through analytics, your population and its health problems. You should know the prevalence for the principal chronic diseases within that area and whether patients are contained within a single community. If you have the idea of creating a pilot program for 1,000 patients with CHF, for example, it will be easier to manage if there is a density of candidates for the program within a small geographic region.

Physician concentration

You will want to explore whether the program will require the involvement of a lot of physicians or just a few. For a payer, it is useful to know whether these 1,000 patients are seen by 500 physicians or 20. And are they specialists or primary care physicians (PCP)? For the payer, it is easier to communicate with, and maintain data from, a small number of physicians. From the providers' perspective, more will be inclined to participate if they have a critical mass of patients who qualify. When any lone payer initiates an effort to create clinical, economic, and administrative ease, a physician or hospital may not be very attentive if only a handful of their patients are members of the plan. Physicians or hospitals are more likely to pay attention if a significant portion of their patient population could be eligible for the program, and if they already are taking care of these patients.

Contained geographic density

You will learn the most if you have a lot of patients in a small geographic area treated by a small number of physicians. You need this regional concentration to create and launch a strong pilot project. These conditions are not always easy to meet. Healthcare delivery often occurs in rural areas and those where just a few of a plan's patients suffer from a particular ailment. These conditions create a difficult environment to launch a successful pilot project. You will learn much more by experimenting in areas of geographic density.

Analyze Before You Start

The next step involves applying data analytics to understand the disease process that is being tackled in the pilot. Through analytics, you will have access to the geographic distribution of the patients with the disease, the providers involved in their care, the severity of the disease at the individual patient level, and the utilization of resources by the patient population with the disease.

Let's take this to the next level and assume that your pilot program is aiming to improve care for 1,000 patients with CHF. The first step is to understand what level of care these patients are currently receiving. You might want to know: What percentage have their disease controlled versus not controlled? Are they on a care plan? What percentage are getting their ejection fractions checked, taking their beta-blockers or angiotensin-converting enzyme inhibitors, and limiting their salt intake?

Although some of this information is available to the payer, much of it will need to come from the provider. Transparency and collaboration begin at this early stage, even before a project is launched. Providers must see it as worthwhile to share information about their patients, including how well their disease is controlled. Although the payer can tell from claims data whether ejection fractions are being checked, the payer most likely will not know the actual results of these tests. Collaboration between a payer and providers is necessary from the very start so that they are both acting on shared information to set meaningful goals.

Next, barriers to care must be assessed. What percentage of patients in your pilot have a PCP? Do they still use the emergency room for most of their primary care needs? If so, why? What barriers are preventing these patients from going to a PCP for this care? Are repeated admissions and readmissions to the hospital occurring? If so, what is driving this high utilization of hospital resources? Are these the same barriers that are driving patients to the emergency room rather than the primary care office? Again, working within a geographically contained population will make it easier to answer these questions.

Finally, you'll want to analyze the financial burden of CHF for these 1,000 patients. Look first at these patients' total healthcare costs. Then look at the areas of service intensity. For example, if the payer is spending, on average, $50,000 per patient per year, is this mostly on hospitalization? What is the emergency room cost? What percentage is spent on primary care? And what about medications?

With this information and analysis, you can create a care delivery road map for these patients. You will know their demographics, which physicians and hospitals are treating them, what their care involves, what this care is costing, how much is being spent in each category, and whether the care is effective, based on readmissions and other utilization data. You can assess how well patients are leveraging the healthcare system, whether their usage is well-optimized or inappropriate, and what barriers to care are driving certain costs.

Now you can define your opportunity and your goals. This is a tactical exercise. The gap between your current situation and the ideal outcome for these patients is your opportunity. Once you define this delta, you are on your way to designing a program. By doing the analysis up front, you know exactly what the starting situation is. From there, you can put together a path and clear line of sight to improvement.

Clinical alignment

No matter what financial goal you have in mind, the first task is to reach clinical alignment by determining and defining the ideal treatment and outcome. The provider and payer must then take the crucial step of agreeing on the clinical goals. Although clinical alignment can take many forms, simplicity is key. For example, you don't want 25 different measures for an asthma patient. You want to pick those that are critical to both the payer and the provider and can be measured easily and accurately. A goal might be to increase from 50% to 80% the proportion of asthma patients who are identified and enrolled in a care management program. Or it might be to increase the percentage of diagnosed asthma patients who are taking aerosol medications properly, or reduce the percentage who are hospitalized in a year.

Evidence-based medicine should serve as the guide for clinical alignment. For example, a hospital might have a six-month readmission rate of 30% for pediatric asthma. But the evidence might show that a certain treatment regimen, combined with patient education, is associated with just 10% readmissions. This suggests that reducing readmissions is a reasonable goal on which to align. Both the payer and provider must agree on the specific goal—perhaps a 15% readmission rate. And they must agree on the clinical path that will be used to get there.

For the 1,000 CHF patients that we've talked about, a goal might include monitoring of ejection fraction over time. Or the clinical goal might be to have all patients control their salt and water intake, or have a certain percentage of patients compliant with their medications. Your pilot will focus on the areas of opportunity that are driving cost, inappropriate utilization of costly resources, and poor outcomes.

Transparency is important here, too. Payer and provider must agree on the clinical goals and how they will be measured. If outcomes are not clearly defined, a provider could ignore best practice guidelines in the quest to bring down cost. The financials would look good, but patient care would suffer. Without a transparent and agreed-upon measure of clinical outcomes, a payer may spend less initially, but it will spend a lot more later on, and quality of care will be hard-hit.

Achieving clinical alignment between payer and provider is the most challenging aspect of creating a pilot project. It requires not only that you agree upon the clinical goals, but also the clinical processes for reaching those goals. Although reaching clinical alignment is the hardest step, it also is the most important. It is the building block of all other forms of alignment. I will devote Chapter 6 to exploring more thoroughly the steps you can take to achieve clinical alignment.

Economic alignment

Delivering the right care, at the right time, in the right setting, will be part of nearly every pilot you can envision. For years, we've seen costs shift to emergency departments and to inpatient care. Many of us are focused on finding ways to shift dollars back into outpatient primary care settings—especially when clinical evidence is clear that outpatient care, primary care in particular, is the best way to preempt chronic diseases. Unfortunately, providing comprehensive medical care at the primary care office to control chronic diseases and prevent disease has not been appropriately financially rewarded in today's reimbursement environment.

Economic alignment seeks to address this problem. It creates a win-win model. The goal is to spend no more than the status quo, while offering providers incentives to keep patients healthier longer. The goal in both the short and long term is to divert patients from critical care and emergency situations.

Let's go back to our CHF patients as an example for how we could introduce economic alignment. Say that the analytics show that each CHF patient costs, on average, $50,000 per year. Of that, $30,000 is spent on hospitalizations and readmissions, $10,000 is spent in the emergency department, and $10,000 in outpatient medical care. This distribution of costs suggests that these patients do not have their CHF under adequate control and that medical care is not well coordinated. A full $40,000 is being spent on the most costly medical services in our industry. This is not to say that all emergency department and inpatient costs can be avoided, particularly in a CHF patient population. However, when the ratio of expenditures is four to one between facility and outpatient care, there is a very strong likelihood for improvement, even among sick populations.

Now, let's say that you set a goal of no more than $25,000 for inpatient and emergency department care. This leaves $25,000 for primary care. This could leave up to $25,000 for primary care and should be spent to stabilize patients' conditions, thereby decreasing the need for inpatient or emergency care. In an economically aligned model, the PCP could opt in to a program that starts by identifying each patient with CHF. The physician could put all of these patients on an evidence-based care plan agreed to in advance with the payer. The payer and provider would align around the concept that patients' needs should be addressed, where possible, through the PCP and not in the emergency room. Together, they could develop a fee schedule that will align them economically toward these goals.

In addition to the primary care fees embedded in the $10,000 per year of outpatient care for each CHF patient, PCPs could now be paid significant fees for identifying all patients with CHF and even larger fees for putting these patients on a care plan and working with them to achieve care plan compliance. Income for PCPs could escalate significantly by doing the right things medically for these patients. The patients, health plans, and providers would all win with such a program.

Physicians and payers would agree, in advance, to the metrics and payment criteria. Now, instead of paying $50,000 per patient, the payer would pay $25,000 for inpatient and emergency care and far greater fees to PCPs—and likely still have a net savings. More importantly, this approach would have far-reaching financial and clinical effects for this patient population, in which disease control—or lack thereof—can profoundly affect medical costs and patient outcomes. Even in the short term, payers would gain significant financial benefits due to this shift from inpatient to outpatient care. These funds could be invested, at least in part, to improve the health and well-being of these patients.

This is one example of economic alignment, in which physicians are paid more to manage patients. Physicians reap rewards not only from the cost savings of diverting patients from the emergency room, but also for the steps they take along the way, such as the care management plan, that ultimately will keep patients healthy. Payers have an economic incentive to offer such an alignment because its total costs will be significantly lower. And the result is better health for the patient.

Although clinical alignment sets a path for the physician and payer, economic alignment adequately compensates the physician for actions that might avoid higher costs down the line. But it also may be in the payer's interest to contribute to the services, staff, or technologies needed to help the provider achieve success. That is where the third prong of the strategy comes in—the administrative alignment.

Administrative alignment

Paying a provider more money to align with preset outcomes is a fine idea, but it will not succeed if the provider does not have the necessary administrative structure and tools in place. In the collaborative model I describe, both payer and provider can contribute to putting in place the administrative tools needed for success. Administrative alignment can be in the form of technology, services, or staff. The provider often knows what type of support would help to reach a clinical goal but lacks the resources, financial or technological, to implement it. Payers have the scale, the resources, and the broad perspective to introduce administrative alignment.

In the CHF scenario described previously, patients who once cost $50,000 would cost less—maybe $45,000 each year. Administrative alignment could mean that a significant portion of the $5,000 difference is reinvested in technologies (such as auto-authorizations or auto-adjudications) that would ease the back-and-forth paperwork of the provider. To some physicians, administrative ease—which lightens their workload or frees them up to see more patients—may be worth as much as the direct financial incentives.

As with all types of alignment, collaboration is essential. Providers need to determine what tools and services will help them and communicate their needs clearly to the payer. For example, a payer might wish to offer financial incentives to physicians who identify all patients with CHF and put them on a care plan. But a provider might not have the ability to do so. The payer, on the other hand, might have data that would help, such as claims data from hospitals showing evidence of CHF. The provider and payer could agree to collaborate.

Alternatively, a physician or clinic might lack the analytics to identify how many CHF patients it is already treating, whereas the payer has data that can help figure that out. So, in this instance, the first step to devising a pilot project for the CHF patient population requires an honest assessment of administrative capabilities and needs by both parties. And it demands the willingness of the providers to work with payers toward alignment.

When creating shared goals, it is incumbent on the payer to ask, "Do you have adequate nursing staff? Could a payer-sponsored 1-800 nurse call line help patients use services more appropriately and help drive the program to success?" The payer could even go a step further and make sure the provider gets useful information about patients who call. Part of the economic alignment might be that the payer charges the provider $1 per month for each patient. But the increased efficiency and improved care would help the provider reach its own outcome goals and help the payer reduce overall costs. In this way, administrative alignment links both clinical and financial factors and makes success possible.

The ideas that I have presented here, and the more in-depth examples of alignment that I will present in subsequent chapters, are intended as starting points for your own creative thinking. Your mission is to consider how these three types of alignment can be applied to the challenges you face. These ideas can be implemented, in whole or in part, with the flavor of the specific region you choose for your experiment. By creating a regional program along the lines of this model, you are likely to see good outcomes and cost savings. Next, we'll look at the tools to bring it all together.

Chapter 4
Tools to Support Collaboration

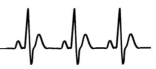

About four years after I started working for my current employer, I received a call from our health plan, checking up on me. My records showed that I, like so many Americans, had been prescribed a medication for high blood pressure. I had been dutifully taking the medication for four years. I answered the nurse's questions: Is your blood pressure controlled? Yes. Do you take your medicine regularly? Yes. Do you have an annual echocardiogram? Yes. Do you control your salt intake? Yes. Check your cholesterol? Yes. For nearly half an hour, she was perfectly on-target and professional in her questions, and I did not begrudge answering them. But was this the best use of the health plan's time and resources?

If the plan's administrators had a view of all the clinical data that my doctor had noted in my chart, they would know that my blood pressure was well-controlled and that my cholesterol levels and echocardiogram were normal. If the plan were connected with my pharmacy records, the administrators would know that I fill my prescription regularly. They would see that I am following my care plan and my condition is well-managed.

I'm not saying it wasn't a worthwhile call. But it probably cost the plan $30. For the best use of the plan's resources, wouldn't it make more sense to call patients who had not received a stress echocardiogram in three years? This information can be found in the plan's own claims data. What if the plan could access key pieces of data from members' medical charts? Instead of calling Dr. Rizk, with the well-controlled blood pressure, the plan could instead call a member whose blood pressure had been creeping upward. And if the plan had a simple interface with the pharmacy, it could find out whose prescription had gone unfilled lately and warranted a call.

Payer-Provider Connectivity

Connectivity in healthcare is defined broadly as the flow of information among all participants—providers, insurers, pharmacies, suppliers, employees, information resources, and consumers.[1] Connectivity—clinical or financial—is one of the most important tools that will enable greater collaboration. Because I focus on the payer-provider relationship, I will address primarily the connectivity between those entities. Keep in mind that I include in the term "providers" everyone who provides care or a service to patients, including pharmacists, nurses, and case managers.

Connectivity in healthcare is just one tool to help us achieve greater alignment. Access to technology that connects payer to provider, provider to provider, and provider to consumer will not automatically solve all the problems in healthcare. Nor must we wait for every piece of technological connectivity to be in place before we can take small but significant steps. For example, even if my plan didn't know the results of my stress echocardiogram because my physician did not provide that information, it would know from the claim that the test was performed. That would distinguish me as a low-priority patient to be called, as opposed to patients who had not been tested in years. Each step we can make toward connectivity—and using that connectivity well—helps improve performance. It is easier to do the right thing when you have the right information, you are the right person to receive it, and it is available at the right time. That is what connectivity is about.

Underuse of connectivity

Evidence of underutilized connectivity abounds. In a recent study by the Commonwealth Fund, only 58% of U.S. patients surveyed who did not have a "medical home" said that their regular doctor seemed informed about the care they received after an emergency room visit.[2] And 29% reported their medical records were not available during a visit or duplicative tests were done.[3] (Medical home, in this case, was defined as "having a regular provider who knows you, is easy to contact, and coordinates your care." I prefer the term "patient-centered, provider-guided medical home" for the model in which a single physician coordinates all aspects of a patient's care.) A basic electronic medical record (EMR) could address many of these issues. But, as of early 2008, only 4% of physicians reported having an extensive, fully functional EMR system, while 13% reported having a basic EMR system.[4]

Despite the available technology, we are far less connected than we could be. There are several reasons for this, but cost is widely regarded as the greatest barrier to implementing most connectivity tools. That is why economic alignment—which includes payer investment in such tools—is so important. Another challenge is persuading providers to use technology that is available to them. Often, the decision-makers in large provider organizations may be a technological generation behind more junior colleagues who grew up at a computer keyboard and readily embrace new technologies. More recently, we're facing a backlash from those who have attempted to adopt an EMR but claim to be disillusioned by an increase in workload and lack of utility. Such frustration is common when EMR implementations do not include connectivity outside of a medical practice. The investment is much more worthwhile if the EMR system can talk to the hospital, other physicians, the pharmacy, the health plan, and so on.

Of the many ways to enhance connectivity, linking payer and provider—particularly the primary care physician (PCP)—is probably the most important in creating the clinical, financial, and administrative alignments we need. But there also are huge rewards to be gained—in efficiency, quality, and provider satisfaction—by linking providers to one another. This need will increase with time.

For example, as I watch the emergence of retail clinics, also called convenient care clinics, I see a great opportunity. We already have a shortage of PCPs, and the problem is expected to grow. Why not leverage these clinics? They can meet some routine needs—cholesterol checks, immunizations, and treatment of minor colds and ear infections—and reduce the burdens on the primary care system. But this will be helpful only if the clinics are connected to PCPs and health plans. In many cases, as these clinics emerge, there has been no sharing of the data they collect. Perhaps a requirement for them should be that each patient interaction be reported to the patient's PCP. If the patient has no PCP, the payer could be alerted.

Connectivity, at its best, can help minimize the duplicative parallel processes and communication gaps that ultimately are so costly and delay diagnosis and treatment. What follows in the next section is my view of connectivity methods that can help align payers and providers. I will address the advantages of each, the challenges to implementation, and how to make the most of your resources as you strive for greater connectivity.

Connectivity Methods

Patients trust their doctors more than they trust their health plans or hospitals. For that reason alone, there is merit to the medical home concept, in which a single provider coordinates a patient's care. Whatever we call it, the model works best when the physician is fully connected. Doctors need data to best manage their patients, but currently they receive information only when they see the patient. There is an ongoing disconnect among the doctor, the health plan, other caregivers, and the hospital. Any element of connectivity that moves actionable data among these key stakeholders is a step toward helping physicians manage care better.

Connecting clinical care electronically

Of the benefits attributed to e-prescribing, the most frequently noted are improved patient safety via a reduction in medication errors and improved efficiency due to fewer phone calls with the pharmacy. But e-prescribing, which uses an automated data-entry process to generate prescriptions and a transmission network to link to participating pharmacies, also is a launching point for very cost-effective connectivity. Consider a 44-year-old patient who always thought of himself as healthy and has no PCP. He suddenly suffers a heart attack. At the emergency room, he is prescribed a beta-blocker. If the beta-blocker were prescribed electronically through a system connected to his health plan, that system could issue an alert that a top-priority drug had been prescribed to an individual without a PCP. The administrator could contact the patient and connect him with a PCP, ideally setting in motion a care management plan for better disease control.

There are ways at getting to this information today, but they rely on patient compliance.

If the patient fills the script for the beta-blocker, then the pharmacy benefit manager can signal the health plan or the health plan can scrub for the pharmacy claim. Timely identification of patients with chronic illness is the foundation of alignment. The sooner such a patient is in a physician's care and on a care plan, the better for the patient and the payer. An e-prescribing tool linked to the plan also could track whether the patient fills a prescription. If a prescription goes unfilled, that patient could be flagged for a follow-up call.

Another tool that is associated with patient safety, but also has huge potential to improve connectivity, is computerized physician order entry (CPOE), an electronic prescribing system that can be used to order labs and tests, as well as prescriptions, usually in the hospital setting. The order integrates with other patient information and laboratory and prescription data, and is automatically checked for potential errors or problems. If shared between provider and payer, the information also can be used to identify patients who need follow-up. Even without a fully interoperative electronic health record (EHR), the information trail left by a CPOE can provide valuable information. (Note that the distinction between EMRs and EHRs will be explained later in this chapter.)

For example, if an unconscious person shows up in the emergency room, a CPOE may contain helpful details from the patient's medical history. A 2005 report noted that fewer than 5% of U.S. hospitals had fully implemented CPOE systems.[5] Up-front costs and resistance from some physicians to using computerized decision-support tools are among the reasons for delays in implementation. CPOE also has the potential to reduce errors that can lead to an inaccurate record of the patient's care and an administrative burden downstream.

Any way you can connect payers and providers is important. Any process that sends clinical information, such as test results, to the payer also is helpful. For example, a payer can tell from a claim that a chest x-ray was done on a patient, but does not see the result. Think how helpful it would be for the payer to know that the result shows pneumonia—and to follow up with the patient. But today, in most cases, the insurer is flying blind, not knowing whether to intervene in a particular case.

Provider-to-provider connectivity also would improve efficiency in how physicians use their time. Typically, a specialist who is referred a patient knows nothing more than a single sentence about why the patient is coming. For physicians to track each other down for a phone conversation to obtain more of the patient's history is very inefficient. Similarly, when a PCP wants to know what a cardiologist thinks about the patient he or she has sent over with complaints of shortness of breath, the PCP doesn't want to make a phone call or ask for a fax to find out what the cardiologist wants to do. PCPs want to be able to access that information on their own time, without having to make a call or a request.

One useful way to promote connectivity is for hospitals to make electronic patient records available to admitting physicians who are outside the hospital's electronic network. Some hospitals allow physicians to access these records from their own office computers. For a patient admitted to the hospital in the morning, the physician can check on labs and order other tests if needed before rounds that afternoon, saving valuable time for all parties. Without that information, the physician would have to be present in the hospital before being able to order additional tests.

When useful information exists that is not shared among providers, you have lost an opportunity. And you have opened the door to inappropriate overuse of re-sources. If a patient moves from one physician to another, the new physician may repeat tests that were already done. If someone enters the emergency room with chest pain, a catheterization may be performed, which would not be necessary if a patient's record of unstable angina were available to the hospital staff members treating him.

Administrative and financial connectivity

One of the most underused connectivity methods is automated transaction connectivity, specifically auto-authorization and auto-adjudication. Making the approval process less cumbersome would save time and resources that could be put to better use. Authorization of services remains a mostly manual, time-draining process involving phone and/or fax.

Consider a physician who deems it necessary to do a procedure on a hospitalized patient. The floor nurse calls the plan for authorization, giving clinical criteria of A, B, and C for that patient to justify medical necessity. A nurse at the plan responds that the plan's clinical rules require clinical criteria D and E as well. So the hospital nurse returns to the physician, who either provides the information to satisfy the criteria, orders additional tests, or gets on the phone to further explain the need for the procedure.

Auto-authorization is the general term for computerized capability to automatically assess medical appropriateness for a requested service and approve or deny that service. A request for authorization for a specific procedure can be submitted electronically and a decision rendered automatically—and immediately—if a set of computer-generated rules are met. The process exists today in varying degrees of sophistication. The most intelligent systems are able to take input from EMRs without the need for any human intervention. Even less sophisticated systems free up clinical staff to spend more time on patient care and improve back-office efficiency. Roughly two-thirds of hospital CEOs surveyed said they expected online auto-authorization systems to enhance revenue and/or bring cost-savings, through better understanding of approval criteria, decreased processing time for staff members, and improved billing.[6]

With auto-adjudication, claims sent electronically by the provider hit a set of rules from the payer and are then processed automatically. This process can enhance alignment, financially and administratively, because payments are more timely and administrative costs in the form of phone calls and faxes are eliminated. This is good for payer-provider relations. Auto-adjudication also offers the potential for huge cost savings. The cost of handling a claim through a paper process is estimated at $6 to $20 per claim. It is in everyone's interest to find an automated way to pay claims accurately.

While a patient is in the office, it often is necessary for a staff member to check a patient's medical eligibility for a visit or test, and what the patient's financial responsibility will be. A long-term goal would be for the entire interaction—from authorization and adjudication—to happen automatically and in real time. That is, when patients are told they need an MRI, they could learn on the spot what locations are approved, how much the insurance will pay of the total, and how much they will be responsible for. And the claim would be processed immediately.

Using current technology, both of the "autos" could be used to align payers and providers economically and administratively, with payers footing the bill for the implementation of the technology. Auto-authorization can be offered as an incentive to providers who comply regularly with practice guidelines for a specific procedure or who are in the top tier for physician compliance overall. I will discuss this further in Chapters 7 and 8.

Electronic patient records

The central tool for tying together a lot of information is the patient record. Distinguishing among the alphabet soup of titles—EMR, EHR, and personal health record (PHR)—is important.

The EMR is an electronic version of a patient's chart, but with the addition of all financial interactions. It resides in the physician's office. A major problem with EMRs is they are not always accessible to all physician practices.

For example, the record of a patient seen by a doctor affiliated with Medical Center A may be accessible to only physicians affiliated with that center. So if the patient goes across town to Medical Center B, the physicians there have no access to the record. This may necessitate an entirely new patient history, which takes time and may not be as accurate or complete as the patient's EMR, which includes the full claims history, such as how many x-rays or CAT scans were performed. Without fully portable electronic records, the data-gathering process becomes inefficient and risks unnecessary duplication of testing.

The limited utility of the EMR may be one reason for its relatively slow adoption—and some physicians' disenchantment with the technology. Some providers have felt that, for an investment of approximately $100,000, they've gotten a cool, searchable patient database tool—instead of paper charts. But often, an EMR doesn't appreciably improve providers' efficiency or quality of care because the EMR is not linked to information they need that exists outside the four walls of their office. Without enough information in the record, an EMR may not seem worth the effort. That said, many practices have done a very good job inserting as much information as possible into their patients' EMRs and have reached a tipping point in efficiency and in monitoring outcomes and delivery of care that they believe improves the quality of care.

The PHR is an electronic record maintained by the patient that usually contains the individual's progress regarding a health challenge such as lowering weight or blood pressure, plus a current medication list. The PHR may or may not be tied into the physician's office for making appointments and renewing prescriptions.

The electronic record with the greatest connectivity potential is the EHR. This document is shared by the health plan and the provider and used as a communication tool between the two parties. With an EHR, a plan may find, through claims, that a patient who had a heart attack is not on a beta-blocker—or that another patient hasn't had a mammogram or flu vaccine. The plan can send a disease registry to the patient's PCP, noting all matters that need to be addressed the next time the patient comes in. Ideally, the physician would respond with information regarding actions taken. The purpose of the EHR is to close gaps in care, minimize disease progression, and maximize chronic disease prevention, which is the main focus.

It is useful for an EHR to connect with e-prescribing data. If a health plan and a pharmacy are connected, even without an EHR, the plan might know that a patient has stopped filling a prescription, which would trigger an alert to contact the patient. But if the EHR were connected to e-prescribing data, the plan administrator might see that the physician stopped the medication for a good reason, such as a hard-to-tolerate side effect. Investing in an EHR makes sense. To achieve full transparency between payer and provider, this is an invaluable tool. However, it does add the potential responsibility for the physician to close all the gaps in care that may be pointed out by the plan. This is where clinical and economic alignment are so crucial. The physician will need to be compensated for the extra work that ultimately will save the plan money through fewer hospitalizations.

Portals

Truly connecting payers and providers requires an electronic vehicle through which all the constituents—the health plan, the physician, and the hospital—can see the same data. This portal needs to contain a patient's history, claims record, all medical tests done, and their results in an easily searchable format.

Thinking back to the example of a hospitalized patient awaiting authorization for a procedure, consider how much time could have been saved for all parties if the floor nurse could have accessed electronically a checklist of what the plan required for authorization. Once that list was complete, he or she could submit the request electronically, without having to make a phone call. This would save time and effort, even in the absence of auto-authorization.

From a provider's perspective, the most effective portal would be multi-payer—that is, the provider would sign in once and be able to access information for each insurer used by his or her patients. Information would be patient-specific, rather than specific to that payer's portal. Although some plans already have what they call portals, they typically lack interoperability. That is, they don't connect to any information outside of their site.

More useful portals are slowly emerging. Some pieces are connected, and some are not. The first success in a fully connected portal, I expect, will come in a single region where the major players have chosen to come together for their mutual benefit. It likely will be a place of geographic density—perhaps a county of 10,000 patients who are covered primarily by one payer. In such an environment, a fully connected portal could really be tested. And once it proves itself, many will see its advantages.

A truly connected portal will enable a provider to submit claims electronically, thus improving the billing cycle. If this process is tied in with auto-authorization, administrative efficiency will increase. And if a portal facilitated e-visits—wherein physicians and patients would engage in secure electronic communication—medical efficiency would increase and patient satisfaction likely would rise. If a physician could use the portal to readily access all patient information and share that information with other providers, then duplicative testing would decrease, time spent on patient care could increase, and quality likely would improve.

The Right Information, to the Right Person, at the Right Time

Gathering the information needed to create EHRs is a challenge. Creating a patient record from bills often starts with imperfect information, because the provider may have billed incorrectly or incompletely. But some health plans are starting with the simplest areas first. Most lab tests, for example, yield data that is relatively easy to enter into an EHR—the number is either normal or not, or either high or low. X-rays and other images are more challenging, because results may be subtle and require a wordy description. And, while one physician or plan may have recent information about a patient, older tests and procedures, or those performed by another provider, may not be available. Finally, there is the matter of timing. We are striving for connectivity in real time. Currently, claims-based information often has a considerable time lag. The faster information can flow between the payer and the provider, the more accurate and actionable it will be.

More important than just the ability for data to flow freely back and forth is the relevance of the data to the person receiving it. It is not effective to give everyone the same data and say, "OK, you decipher through it." Information is most meaningful if it is routed to the people who need it to make a decision. Distributed work flow technologies are tools that allow for this kind of information distribution. Health plans use these work flow tools to push information out to providers with the intent of meaningful actions, enhanced collaboration, and transparency.

An early example of this practice occurred after a deluge of media reports focused on lives that might have been saved if women received mammograms. Health plans began experimenting with alerts to members when they were due for a mammogram. This connectivity may have been relatively low-tech, but it started the practice of actionable information being shared among stakeholders.

Ultimately, we will see connectivity that goes beyond telling the physician that a patient is due for a flu vaccine or mammogram. True connectivity will occur when a well-managed diabetes patient unexpectedly has a significantly abnormal test result during a routine visit. The patient might not normally be scheduled to return for a month. But if the lab conveys the test result quickly and directly to the plan, the plan could alert the doctor and patient about the importance of a follow-up visit, and, meanwhile, engage the patient with education. Without such a system, the plan normally wouldn't engage the patient with education until after it learned the lab values from the physician (which might not be transmitted) or saw that the patient filled a prescription for insulin (perhaps indicating a progression of disease). Progressive health plans will screen for this information, so that if an important lab value shows up as abnormal, there is immediate action.

Distributed work flow also means pushing information to the people who are most suited to act upon it. A plan might see that a diabetes patient has not received diabetes counseling and might check the practice's profile to see whether it offers this service. Because we know that people trust health information most when it comes from their physician, it is ideal that such counseling be provided by that practice. So, rather than attempt to arrange for the patient to receive the plan's counseling program, the plan would alert the practice to offer counseling the next time the patient came in. Because the practice has the most access to that patient and the capability, it would be the best entity to perform the task.

Who Should Pay, and Who Should Lead?

The cost of implementing new technologies is an important part of economic alignment, yet many technologies are underutilized because the stakeholders are not aligned. Ultimately, these investments will pay for themselves, thanks to the efficiencies they introduce, even before they provide the longer-term benefits of better management of chronic disease. The initial investment will come from a stakeholder who stands to benefit from the new technology. For practical purposes, it almost always will be the plan that has the resources to initiate connectivity. Large hospitals and hospital systems may have the means to do it, and may be in a position to launch pilot projects around connectivity technology. As with all alignment, the tools of connectivity should be provided in exchange for agreed-upon performance goals.

A lot of good technology exists, and payers have put many sophisticated systems into place. But much of it is piecemeal. Instead of creating more systems that don't talk to each other, it may be the role of the payer to bring information together. This can happen best region by region, rather than through some sweeping national mandate. In most regions, financial connectivity is ahead of clinical connectivity because of the real, immediate dollars involved. But even in areas with clinical connectivity, it will be up to the payer to take the lead in collecting the data, making sense of it, and routing it in the right direction.

Connectivity cannot guarantee that people will abruptly change behaviors and make the right decisions. But connectivity is a critical enabler. It is easier to do the right thing and to make better decisions with the right tools.

ENDNOTES

1. Regina Herzlinger and Alfred Martin, "Connectivity in Healthcare," Harvard Business School note, copyright © 2008, 2006 President and Fellows of Harvard College.

2. Schoen, et al, 2007 Commonwealth Fund International Health Policy Survey, "Higher-Performance Health Systems," *Health Affairs* 26, 6 (October 31, 2007): 32, *www.commonwealthfund.org/usr_doc/Schoen_intlhltpolicysurvey2007_chartpack.pdf?section=4056* (accessed December 13, 2008).

3. Schoen, et al, 2007 Commonwealth Fund International Health Policy Survey, "Higher-Performance Health Systems," *Health Affairs* 26, 6 (October 31, 2007): 28, *www.commonwealthfund.org/usr_doc/Schoen_intlhltpolicysurvey2007_chartpack.pdf?section=4056* (accessed December 13, 2008).

4. DesRoches, et al., "Electronic Health Records in Ambulatory Care—A National Survey of Physicians," *New England Journal of Medicine* 359: (July 3, 2008): 50–60, *http://content.nejm.org/cgi/content/full/359/1/50* (accessed December 13, 2008).

5. The Leapfrog Group, "Computerized Physician Order Entry Factsheet," The Leapfrog Group, factsheet, revision April 9, 2008, *www.leapfroggroup.org/media/file/Leapfrog-Computer_Physician_Order_Entry_Fact_Sheet.pdf* (accessed January 25, 2009).

6. Deloitte, "The Future of Health Care 2005: The Survey," 11, *www.deloitte.com/dtt/cda/doc/content/the%20future%20of%20Health%20Care(1).pdf* (accessed December 13, 2008).

Chapter 5
Leading a Successful Partnership

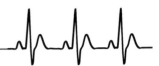

We've talked about connectivity in the technological sense. In this chapter, I will address an essential human factor needed to promote connectivity: leadership. To create a new partnership of payers and providers, we need strong leaders from every quarter. These leaders must have the vision and knowledge to bring about change. But, beyond qualifications of rank, knowledge, and experience, the leaders who will produce change must have the traits necessary to bring people and programs together. In this chapter, I will spell out a vision for leadership. I will also discuss how to structure a collaborative effort and establish the work flows and accountability necessary for a collaboration to succeed.

Create a Small but Powerful Governance Group

A successful partnership begins with governance. Once you define your region, your target population, and your general goals for a collaborative pilot project, the next step is to put in place a governing body. Generally, this governance group should include two senior leaders from each of your three key constituencies: payer, physician group, and hospital. That decision will depend on how clear you are at the outset about your project's goals. In most cases, the governance group can be invaluable in assisting and gathering the information you need to define a sound and worthwhile project.

A project must have buy-in at the top of the organization from the very start. Therefore, the health plan's chief medical officer (CMO), who may have initiated the project, is a key player and should hold a seat on the governing body. As a physician, the CMO has a medical approach that is practical and effective for quality of care. And more importantly, he or she is well aware of the needs of the population being served. The CMO should also understand the mind-set of the physicians in the community as well as having credibility with these physicians.

The president, chief financial officer (CFO), or chief operating officer (COO) might hold the second seat for the plan. Alternatively, the seat could go to the plan's top data analytics expert, who will play a crucial role in the project. The credibility and validity of information is essential. What data to collect, the collection process, how it's reported, and actionable steps will follow from the analysis of that data—essentially, pinpointing the best programs to align the team and support management strategies.

On the physician side, governance seats should be occupied by physicians in existing leadership roles, such as a physician leader or medical director of a physician group. If the physicians are based at an academic medical center, one seat should be filled by a dean or well-regarded department chair, because these individuals represent the highest-ranking physicians in the organization. Their involvement will send a message to other physicians that the project is to be taken seriously.

From the hospital system, one seat should be occupied by a senior executive, be it the CEO, COO, or CFO. A good choice for the remaining hospital seat is the chief information officer, who will provide much-needed expertise on current and future technologies necessary to support the project and/or interoperability between systems (hospital, health plan, and physicians).

Changing the model of care will involve unprecedented sharing of information and alignment around common goals. To meet this challenge, the most senior leadership from each constituency must champion the project, generate momentum within their organizations, and remove obstacles to collaboration. Most importantly, members of the governance team must have the authority to make swift decisions—especially those with economic impacts—on behalf of their organizations and ensure that those decisions are honored. This is a critical factor in the success of the project.

It may be tempting to build an army-sized governing body to cover all perspectives of the healthcare landscape and concerns of each constituency. But I strongly recommend limiting your governance group to the six to seven individuals described previously. We've learned through the experience of Community Health Information Networks that bigger is not necessarily better. You need a handful of individuals who, together, have strong skills in medicine, administration, data, technology, and finance. Smaller is better than bigger, in my view. The leadership governance group also need not be perfectly balanced with counterparts from each constituency. Competencies can be leveraged; for example, the CFO of a health plan or hospital system could provide financial discipline and oversight for the entire project, rather than having three CFOs in the project's governance body.

Once the project begins, it is important that each member of the leadership group leave his or her organization's interests at the door of the meeting room. It is in this small group that trust must begin. The leadership governance should see itself as a group of knowledgeable, empowered individuals with a shared problem to solve. The alignment must begin in that room.

Select an outstanding leader

The first job of the leadership governance is to appoint a single, accountable person to lead the project. This "team lead" will make sure the project stays focused on the objective and that real solutions are developed, despite any hurdles or conflicts the group encounters. The team lead will also be available to members from any of the three constituencies on a day-to-day basis. Once the project is under way, the team lead will keep the rest of the group informed, ideally with relevant monthly reports.

I envision the team lead as a strong physician executive from either the plan or the provider side. This person needs to be a true believer in the value of the project and must be driven to achieve success; he or she is the champion of the project. This person must be financially savvy, understand sound delivery of care, be comfortable with conflict, attuned to the needs of all constituencies, and willing to roll up his or her sleeves and become engrossed in the project. This physician leader needs to have a vision for care that is continuum-based rather than episodic, with an approach toward chronic illness that is both creative and practical. He or she can balance the value of new medical interventions with cost-effectiveness and quality of care.

The physician leader should be well-rounded; a general practice background may be more useful than the experience of specialty practice. Although a specialist might be able to lead the kind of change we are talking about, he or she would need to have a track record of neutrality rather than being tied to his or her specialty's point of view. (For example, it would be unfortunate to have a team lead trained in endocrinology who then requires each diabetic patient to see an endocrinologist.) It is also important that the team lead be comfortable with technology—not only with using information technology himself or herself, but advocating for its use among other physicians.

It seems obvious that the team lead should be a collaborator by nature—someone who already has grasped the necessity of bringing all parties together for innovation. The individual must also have shed the traditional view of payers and providers each protecting their own turf. The team lead must go beyond the linear thinking of traditional problem-solving to embrace the multiple dimensions involved in bringing about change.

Identify goals

As soon as the governance group is assembled and a leader appointed, it must ask itself two questions:

- Where do we sense the greatest need for improvement?

- What data do we need to make decisions?

For example, let's say the group decides that the greatest need is to improve the management of diabetic patients. Each constituency would then bring forth its own data to help assess the situation, including claims data from the health plan, data from the hospitals regarding diagnosis-related groups, and clinical data from the physicians. The team might see, from the physician data, that 50% of diabetic patients are uncontrolled; from the hospital data, that this leads to a specific number of hospitalizations; and, from the plan data, the average cost associated with these patients. The governance group identifies the pain points of each constituency—physician, hospital, and plan—and, as a group, defines its target clinical and bottom-line outcomes. For example, it might seek to improve the health of diabetic patients.

Once the target is identified, the group must devise clinical goals that are acceptable to all, such as achieving a 90% medication compliance rate among the previously uncontrolled diabetics. The group must achieve consensus regarding how to manage the patients, what benchmarks will be used to assess progress, and what data will be examined when. Creating transparency is a major part of the job, and the team lead must see to it that channels exist for the appropriate information to be shared among physicians, hospitals, and the health plan, as well as to and from pharmacists and case managers.

The team lead also begins the process of creating economic alignment, first by gathering from each constituency its ideas about equitable financial arrangements. Defining cost-saving goals for the plan and compensation targets for the providers is an inevitable challenge that will require strong leadership to overcome. All involved must accept that with innovation comes risk. A pilot project is intended to show what may or may not work. The goal is to experiment, using a tactical and business-oriented approach.

There is no surefire road map for the next step in structuring a pilot program, but it's important that leaders tackle the project systematically, one step at a time. For example, the group might choose to start by creating a technology working group to ensure the ability to share data. The most important step is to commit to move forward with the project and get started. As you work, you will get smarter. Some organizations hold themselves back out of fear of the unknown. They may feel a need for more partners to share the risk or provide additional expertise. But most organizations don't realize the extent of their capabilities. Once a leadership group comes together, an organization will see more clearly what needs to be done. The model will evolve.

Three Work Streams

To get a project under way, you need to organize three work streams—the analytical, clinical, and process work streams. Each stream creates a critical pathway to defining your project and a path for execution throughout the project. The team lead is the central point to bring the three work streams together.

The analytical work stream

The analytical work stream includes the data-gathering required to obtain a holistic view of the problem to be tackled and to define the pilot project, as described previously and in Chapter 2. Once the project is defined, this work stream includes asking and answering questions such as:

- What data will be used throughout the project?

- Who will receive the different information sets that will be generated?

- How often will the data need to be analyzed and distributed?

- In what format should the information be presented?

Going back to our example of diabetic patients, the analytical work stream would involve analyzing the diabetic population in terms of its utilization of medical services and pharmacy compliance. Those responsible for the analytical work stream would present this information to the appropriate project team members.

The clinical work stream

The clinical work stream begins with agreeing upon desired outcomes, often using evidence-based medicine as a guide. This work stream defines the path on which those patients will be placed to achieve desired outcomes. You might define different paths for patients of varying needs. For example, diabetic patients with a glucose level of 160 mg/dl might be on a different clinical path than patients whose level exceeds 300 mg/dl. The clinical guidelines might specify how frequently blood glucose monitoring should occur, the degree of patient education necessary, which staff will handle which issues, and the clinical goals.

The process work stream

The third, and perhaps simplest, work stream is the process work stream. This work stream creates the infrastructure for how the project will proceed. Some of the questions to be resolved include:

- How will we divide the patients among the physicians involved?

- What administrative support—such as a disease management program or a 1-800 call line—will help physicians reach the desired goals?

For example, if physicians say a call line would be helpful, the process work stream needs to establish information to be relayed from the call line nurse to the physician. Too often, there are no guidelines for this type of communication. For instance, if a patient calls a 1-800 nurse line because his or her blood sugar is 300 mg/dl, the physician needs to be informed of the call and whether the patient was instructed to take his or her insulin and monitor the sugar level again. A process must be put in place for appropriate follow-up.

Another example of a process work stream task would be if the project's designers decided it would be helpful to know whether a patient discharged from a hospital had filled his or her prescriptions within a certain time frame. The process work stream would first need to establish connectivity with the pharmacy and decide who should receive prescription information—the hospital, the primary care physician, or the plan. Next, the process work stream would determine who is responsible for acting on the information and/or contacting the patient.

Create an Accountability Map

A crucial concept is what I call "accountability mapping." This really just comes down to "What do you do, and what do I do?" and "Who provides the tools to do it?" In a collaborative world, accountability mapping helps you make the most of the resources a payer and provider can offer. It eliminates duplication and closes gaps in care. As you map accountability, you deconstruct the care process. Once you define all the processes that need to take place in each, payer and provider agree on who is responsible for what. The governance group may set the general strategies, but it will be up to the operational group to move forward on them.

I see accountability mapping breaking down into three areas: identification, management, and measurement. In any effort toward alignment between payer and provider, the first area to map is identification of patients and desired outcomes. Both payer and provider would have to agree on what data elements are needed to get started and who will be responsible for providing that data. For example:

- Clinical data are needed and will be provided by the physician

- Historical data are needed and will be provided by the payer

- The desired outcome will be identified collaboratively between the payer and the provider

Next, provider and payer must map accountability for patient management. For patients with congestive heart failure, accountability mapping would answer questions such as:

- What is the care plan?

- What is the infrastructure for patient management?

For example, if a heart failure patient's at-home weigh-in shows a five-pound gain over 36 hours, should he call the physician or a 1-800 line? Who pays for the 1-800 line? Who follows up on the call—the physician or the plan? Who provides patient education—the physician's office or the payer? Is the content of the patient education consistent with the information given on the 1-800 line?

Third, you need to map accountability for measurement. For example:

- In patient care, how often will intermittent outcome goals be measured?

- What data will be collected and by whom?

- At what intervals will that data be shared?

Traditionally, each constituency has kept its own data in silos inaccessible to others. Once project planning determines a need for certain data to be shared, and the process work stream includes that data as part of the metrics, there must be accountability that the data exchange occurs in a timely and appropriate manner. Some examples would be:

- Can a hospital provide real-time readmission data to a payer?

- Can a physician provide the value of a hemoglobin A1c test to a plan, so that the plan can monitor the level of disease control for diabetic patients?

- Can a pharmacist inform a payer or provider whenever a prescription is filled?

The key is to determine clearly who is responsible for what. This must be mapped out and articulated in a way transparent to those involved.

In the unaligned world, payers and providers all too often duplicated services—possibly each having their own case manager, who might have told the same patient conflicting information. Maybe a 1-800 call line was in place, but no one was handling follow-up. The goal of accountability mapping is to diminish parallel and conflicting processes, while also identifying gaps in care that could lead to costly problems in the future.

It takes strong leadership to initiate collaboration where there has been none. But this is the only way we can align our healthcare system to bring the efficiencies that will contain our costs and deliver better care. The next three chapters will look in greater detail at specific ways to achieve alignment.

What Makes a Leader?

When I think about leadership, I remember the day I heard a true luminary in the payer world address a room full of physicians and hospital executives. He began his talk with these words: "So what will it take for you guys to stop robbing me?!"

Here was a person I respected greatly, extraordinary in his knowledge of health insurance. Yet, as I listened to his words, and saw the grimaces in the crowd, it was clear to me that the old paradigm of confrontational leadership will not move us forward as an industry.

A leader today needs to be a collaborator. He or she must be able to seek input from many sides and then be willing to change, where appropriate, his or her own thinking based on new information. Gone are the days when a CEO or other top leader could make a decision and throw it to his staff members to figure out how to implement it. There is a need today for leaders who can build consensus—first in their own organization, be it a medical group, a hospital, or a health plan. Given the challenges within healthcare, today's leaders must also create consensus outside their organizations. It is only through the ability to see a problem from many vantage points that we can build a fruitful alignment among parties that traditionally have been at odds with each other.

This is not to say that a collegial personality is all that is needed. True leaders in healthcare today have a clear vision of a sensible and achievable final outcome. They are willing to innovate to get there—to drive their organization, and their collaborators, to that level of alignment. Today's leaders must be analytical, tactical, and execution-oriented. They engage in tactical execution and pay attention to the details; they do not just present pie-in-the-sky ideas.

On the health plan side, we need leaders who can see the big picture for the entire healthcare delivery system. It's no longer a matter of "us" versus "them" in terms of who gets to the finish line first or meets certain financial targets for the quarter. Any solution needs to work for all parties involved. Instead of "us" and "them," the thinking needs to be "all of us." True leaders are building systems that work for all constituencies—not just for today, but also for tomorrow.

I am encouraged to see a new breed of physician leaders who are willing to look at business squarely. They embrace new technologies that optimize time and medical knowledge. There is a need for such physicians in leadership positions across the industry. There may be industries in which strong leaders can transport their skills from one industry to another because commonalities exist. But that is less often true in healthcare.

The intricacies of patient care make it particularly difficult to adapt effectively when coming from the outside. Understanding how care is delivered at the patient level is very important and provides leaders with a powerful view of what needs to be accomplished. This is not to say that only physicians can be successful in leadership roles. However, nonphysicians, if they are to be effective, must develop a deep understanding of how patient care is delivered. When a physician is involved in policymaking, the resulting decisions are typically more adaptable in the real world of practicing medicine.

The type of leadership I am describing is not like a set of new clothes that you can get up in the morning and try on. It is a way of thinking and acting. Credibility comes from your track record of successful results. It also comes from your manner of dealing with colleagues in your organization and across the industry. Some people might say that how a person communicates is just a matter of style and temperament. But I think it is much more than that. The words and tone you choose for a particular situation are a reflection of your judgment and leadership. Positive and respectful communication creates the opportunity for leadership.

There are many paths and many mechanisms to success, but there is no room for arrogance if your goal is collaboration.

Chapter 6
Clinical Processes for Greater Cooperation

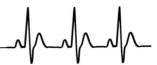

Clinical alignment is the cornerstone of all the other types of alignment. As such, it is the basis of a new model for payer-provider relations. But reaching clinical alignment is not easy. This is not surprising when you consider that even among physicians there is often disagreement about the best course of treatment for a particular problem.

The first challenge of any pilot project is to define the clinical area—diabetes, hypertension, or something else—it will align around. The next step, and perhaps the hardest, is to achieve consensus among all constituents on best practice clinical guidelines (align around how medical care will be delivered to achieve the desired outcomes, specifically treatments that will be emphasized and scrutinized; patient behaviors that will be reinforced or discouraged; activities that physicians and other care team members will focus on). Last, providers must implement what is agreed upon. If payers and providers agree to use the same set of rules for clinical alignment, and providers feel there is transparency in how they are being measured, then economic and administrative alignments can be realized to bring about true alignment. To me, true alignment means an equitable solution for all parties that balances the needs of each and has everyone working to achieve agreed-upon medical and financial goals.

Aligning Around Evidence

Clinically aligning around the evidence should be easy, right? Good research may conclude that it is more effective to treat patients one way rather than another for a particular problem. But it is not always so simple. Of the vast number of potential medical questions that may arise, evidence-based research exists for relatively few. Fortunately, many of the same medical questions occur with great frequency. For some conditions, evidence-based medicine (EBM) provides pathways of treatment. For others, professional and specialty societies have developed standards of practice. But for medical problems that are addressed by multiple specialties, standards might differ from one specialty to the next. And even within one professional group, regional variations might exist. The result is that physicians might vary a great deal in how they treat a given problem.

Clinical decision-support tools based on EBM and standards of medical practice can be immensely helpful in bringing consistency to the delivery of care. They are used by health plans and the government to define appropriate acceptance or denial of a claim, and hospitals use them to anticipate whether a health plan will pay or deny for an admission. Although many physicians understand that these clinically based criteria are a way to communicate and codify standards of care, they remain underutilized by physicians. Even if clinical guidelines are readily accessible in print or electronic format, physicians tend to refer to them only occasionally. For example, when a patient comes in with chest pain, few physicians turn to their electronic decision-support tool to decide whether to do invasive testing. They make their decisions based on how they were trained, standards in their community, and the guidance and leanings from their professional associations.

Throughout the years of mistrust, when payers and providers worked to outmaneuver each other, each tried to prevent the other from knowing exactly how decisions were made—both medically and financially. Sharing information was like handing the other side their playbook. Now, we have come to realize that, for the sake of efficiency and cost management, we must operate from the same playbook. This is why clinical alignment is important. It is not enough to simply know each other's rules for decision-making. Actual agreement to shared rules, in advance, is essential to slowing cost escalation. Clinical alignment must be tactical, on-the-ground, and transparent. The challenges to clinical alignment are to reach agreement on inclusion and exclusion criteria, come to consensus on the best course of treatment, allow for regional differences, and create a path for physicians to make exceptions.

The evidence is so clear for some interventions, and the outcomes so measurable, that no one can deny the benefits. For example, we know that if every patient who has had a myocardial infarction (MI) were put on a beta-blocker, it would save 4,400–5,600 lives per year. If cholesterol were managed within the range recommended by the American Heart Association, we would save 10,000–17,000 lives per year. Controlling blood pressure would save 56,000–98,000 lives. Controlling hemoglobin A1c would save 2,000–3,400 lives. Combining these four basic protocols would save between 73,000 and 124,000 lives annually. These interventions are very easy to align around.

Setting Clinical Goals

Since basic interventions to control heart disease and diabetes are ripe for alignment, any one or combination of them is suitable as the basis for a pilot project. Payers and providers must choose an easily quantifiable goal for the outcome they are trying to reach—be it simply a percentage of patients who are identified or put on a care plan, or a percentage of patients with a certain level of disease control. To start determining a quantifiable goal, examine the relevant data for a particular population at the outset and compare it with known data on achievable outcomes. Analytical tools to measure health status and utilization are crucial, yet these capabilities remain underutilized and underleveraged.

For example, health plans are focusing much attention on chronic disease control measures such as hemoglobin A1c—a powerful indicator of the level of control of diabetes. A physician and a health plan might measure the percentage of diabetes patients they share who are currently having hemoglobin A1c testing, as prescribed by evidence. To gather more meaningful data, they might develop a profile for the provider that includes the percentage of eligible patients who are undergoing the test as indicated, the percentage of those tested who are under good control, and the percentage who are not.

The most basic scenario for clinical alignment is a program in which physicians are paid to identify members with chronic disease, put them on a treatment plan, and work toward a predetermined, measurable goal for that category of patients. This could mean that the physician identifies all hypertensive patients and inputs them into a database; prescribes the appropriate first-line drug(s), such as a diuretic and, if needed, an angiotensin-converting enzyme inhibitor; sees each patient twice yearly; and achieves adequate blood pressure control. Each step would trigger a prenegotiated payment.

For a hospital system, alignment could be as simple as teaming up with a plan that has a population of 10,000 people within its geographic range on a simple measure for reducing readmissions after an MI. For instance, the health plan and the hospital could agree that every patient who leaves the hospital after an MI must be on a beta-blocker. When the hospitals demonstrate they have achieved this goal after a predetermined timeline, they would automatically receive a predetermined payment.

Every attempt at clinical alignment will be unique, shaped by the circumstances of a particular population and the local healthcare community's resources and needs. But the benefits are universal—to simultaneously improve quality, control costs, and improve patient health.

Consider what happened when a community health center in Bradenton, FL, introduced the medical home concept. The center connected each patient to a personal physician or nurse practitioner, increased hours of operation to include weekends, and trained staff to work in patient-care teams. As reported by the Commonwealth Fund, the wait for well-child visits dropped from 14 days to less than one day, and office wait times decreased. But, most significantly, hospitalizations for children dropped dramatically, from approximately 1,800 to 775 per year.[1] Although a cost analysis was not included in the report, one can imagine the financial benefits of the reduced hospitalizations. This was a local solution to a local problem, which is the key to solving our challenges in healthcare.

Possibilities for informal clinical alignment

Clinical alignment also can be accomplished outside a formal pilot program. Either a payer or provider could initiate collaboration in an area plagued by bureaucratic back-and-forth over claims. Consider the example of hospital admissions. Over time, hospital associations have developed their own set of criteria for admission, while payers either purchase or design their own criteria for what is and is not authorized. The result is that each side is more reactive than proactive when dealing with the other.

It is conceivable that a hospital system with 80% of its patients coming from two health plans could approach those health plans and propose that they come to agreement for a certain condition regarding:

- Situations that require hospitalization

- Reasonable guidelines and expectations for admission lengths of stay

- Patient conditions that must be met for a discharge

Alternatively, payers and providers could instead seek agreement on criteria for various levels of intensity within a hospitalization—intensive care, telemetry, surgery, and discharge. They could start with just one condition. For example, they could determine that a heart failure patient needs to have predetermined improvements in cardiac and lung function to move from the ICU to telemetry. The hospital and health plan could also agree on a clear protocol for discharge that includes a follow-up plan, identifies who will execute the plan, describes how the primary care physician (PCP) will be notified of the discharge, and outlines the role the PCP will play in ensuring a smooth transition of care. Both the insurer and the hospital stand to benefit from this clarified, unified method of managing admissions.

Such collaboration also eliminates an enormous amount of costly bureaucracy for all parties. Much less time would be wasted on claims submission, reauthorization, and administration.

It's important to keep alignment simple. We cannot expect all parties to agree on everything under the sun. Rather, a strategic collaboration begins with focusing on a few of the most relevant issues for both parties. Through clear, small wins, they can gain the internal and external buy-in needed for current and future success. Looking at the example of hospital admissions, all parties might set forth up front that they will not attempt to make medications part of the agreement. Alignment on medication is surely important, but it might be too much to tackle initially. Attempting to solve every unaligned area at the outset will only bog a project down, perhaps fatally.

Why Clinical Agreement Does Not Come Easily

A challenge to alignment is the many areas of medicine in which guidelines do not exist or there is not complete agreement among physicians about the best clinical course. When a new therapeutic is introduced, rarely is there enough evidence accumulated to determine its optimal use. So a plan tries to reach internal consensus, and physician groups try to do the same. Such is the case today in the budding area of genomic medicine, in which plans are deciding what tests they will pay for and under what circumstances. Even for therapeutics that have been available for a while, we still see considerable differences in practice patterns depending on geography, physician specialty, and individual preference. It is especially challenging for payer and provider to align when there is not clinical consensus.

If we were starting from scratch in the payer-provider relationship, we would create a world in which there were no regional or specialty differences in practice patterns. In a world where clinical decisions (and the expenses they generate) were the same for every two identical diagnoses, plans could easily model expenses against actuarial data.

However, uniformity of practice, and uniformity of patients, is not reality. This leads to discord between payers and providers. Payers look at the disparate treatments across the United States and may conclude that providers lack the discipline to incorporate best evidence into how they practice medicine. Providers chafe against pressure to conform to a single treatment protocol for a medical condition, saying that human biology is far too complex for such a simplistic approach. The real answer is somewhere in the middle.

Understanding why differences exist in clinical practice helps us get past them and achieve clinical alignment. A fascinating tool for looking at variations in U.S. health-care is the Dartmouth Atlas (*www.dartmouthatlas.org*). It documents, using Medicare data, variations in how medical resources are distributed and used across the United States. It not only shows that medical practice varies greatly from one geographic region to the next, but also that variations exist within regions. For instance, within a relatively small geographic area, patients diagnosed with prostate cancer are treated differently—surgery versus radiation—depending on their ZIP code.

We also have to acknowledge that two very different treatments may lead to nearly identical outcomes. Let's consider two similar heart attack patients. One may have surgery and a stay in the ICU, costing $30,000, and the other may be treated much less aggressively with medication, for a total cost of $10,000. Despite the stark differences in treatment and expense, both patients may survive and achieve similar health status. Naturally, both physicians involved would believe that their course of treatment was optimal, and would offer it to the other patient if the opportunity arose. This is one of the most confounding truths of medicine, and it leads to great difficulty in setting practice guidelines.

Variations in clinical care, and the intensity of care, often are associated with whether the physician is a PCP or a specialist. Some chronic conditions can be treated by either, depending on the healthcare market and other factors. If guidelines from the American College of Cardiology differ from those of the American Academy of Family Physicians for treating a specific aspect of heart disease, two patients with identical problems may receive different tests and therapies, depending on who is treating them. Some conditions may fall to two specialties, with each specialty taking a different approach. If a prostate cancer patient sees a radiation specialist, he likely will be treated with radiation; if he sees a urologist, he is more likely to have his prostate surgically removed. A PCP who initially diagnoses the condition may be in the habit of referring to one specialist or the other. Sometimes availability of resources can also affect clinical treatment. In some communities, an abundance of urologists might drive high surgical rates. In other communities, radiation therapy might dominate because large radiation therapy centers are easily accessible.

Even within a single specialty, doctors are trained regionally, which leads to regional patterns in practice. Physicians take with them into practice the decision-making processes that they learn in medical school and residency. How care delivery is structured in a region also affects treatment patterns. An invasive cardiologist trained in the Northeast may work differently than one in the West, where managed care has had a greater effect on practice patterns. For example, the use of invasive cardiology procedures, such as coronary stents, is more prevalent in the Northeast than in the West.

Alignment Does Not Mean One Size Fits All

Providers often assume that if two treatments have the same result, payers always will steer care toward the least expensive treatment, instituting mandates and incentives for physicians to take the less costly approach. But to reach true clinical alignment, payers must consider the variations in how physicians practice and work with them, customizing their approach to the region and practice patterns.

Therefore, working regionally is the best way to come up with solutions that are practical. It is not practical for a payer to insist on a certain treatment by every provider nationwide—even if warranted by the evidence—if the treatment is unpopular in that region. Nor is it practical to expect physicians and hospitals throughout the state of California to abide by a process just because that's how it is done in Boston, or vice versa.

Let's return to the example of prostatectomy versus radiation. It would be unworkable for a plan to require that every enlarged or cancerous prostate be removed surgically. Physicians who favor radiation are working from evidence that shows the benefits of radiation. Those who favor surgical removal also are working from credible EBM. If a plan puts together a national guideline that it will not reimburse for radiation therapy, it will alienate radiation oncologists—and vice versa for urological surgeons, if the guideline does not reimburse for surgical removal. This is also a good example of a condition in which patient preference regarding the pros and cons of each approach needs to be factored into guidelines.

Similarly, if a plan says it will pay for intensive rehab for lower back pain but not for back surgery, it will alienate the entire constituency of spine surgeons, who would have reason to regard the plan as inflexible and unreasonable. When evidence for two procedures is equal, or close, a payer's willingness to work with local providers is a step toward a trusting relationship.

Therefore, alignment must reflect the needs and habits of the region. So if the outcomes of two clinical paths are essentially equal, a plan should align with the medical leanings of the region and allow it.

For example, let's consider a patient with chest pain. A nuclear medicine echocardiogram and a cardiac catheterization will provide important information about how to manage the patient. Evidence shows that the echocardiogram is a much more cost-effective initial step, with no clinical drawbacks. However, in some markets, the first mode of action is catheterization. As long as the practice is not abusive, the financial disparity is not huge, and the clinical benefits equal, it may not be effective for health plans to insist on the most cost-effective process.

That is why the same national health plan may cover prostate radiation in Florida and removal in Boston for the same kind of prostate tumor. Even in situations in which the outcomes are different—but not hugely so—accommodating regional preferences is a reasonable step toward alignment.

Evidence + Flexibility = Trust

One big caveat is that there must be checks and balances against use of an expensive test or treatment that is no more effective than a less costly one. And it will not be possible for every guideline to keep each medical specialty society happy. However, where the evidence exists, payers and providers need to align around it as a rule. Where the evidence is less clear, it is up to payers and providers to collaborate and allow for flexibility.

Clinical alignment between the payer and provider can be edited or customized to unique circumstances. This may occur due to lack of evidence that matches the population in question, or lack of resources. For example, even if research suggests it is prudent to require an MRI before a certain procedure, this is not a reasonable requirement in a rural community that is 100 miles from the nearest MRI machine.

For true collaboration and trust to exist, providers must know that any clinical content is subject to tailoring and agreement on the part of physicians. Payer and provider must collaborate in modifying and customizing a decision-making tool.

This is as true for a plan's clinical guidelines as it is for order sets for doctors and hospitals. Typically, the payer's medical director(s) work with provider representatives to determine that one treatment is more appropriate than another, in certain circumstances. Those in the business of creating guidelines have learned that one route to success is to involve the most skeptical members of each constituency—especially physicians—in this collaboration process.

Providers are naturally skeptical about the people who control their payments, and they do not believe that payers' incentives are always aligned with patients' best interests. Credibility and transparency are crucial to easing those concerns and developing trust. Any guidelines must be based on very sound clinical principles, with a strong evidence base to support the position.

For example, if a payer is perceived as rushing patients out of the hospital, caregivers will assume it is for cost reasons. But if a payer shares data showing that the risks of hospital-acquired infections exceed the benefits of an extra inpatient day, the discussion can be focused—as it should be—on clinical integrity and safety.

Payers and providers must share information to engender trust, a crucial first step. When both parties make their information transparent and seek each other's feedback, they can move forward together. The cornerstone of any improvement plan is that it define appropriate care for a clinical situation and reach consensus on what steps will be taken to provide that care.

ENDNOTE

1. Melinda Abrams of the Commonwealth Fund, at 2008 McKesson Healthcare Leadership Forum, May 15, 2008, Williamsburg, VA.

Chapter 7
Economic Alignment: The Right Incentives

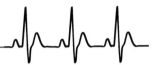

We now know how important it is for payers and providers to align around clinical goals and outcomes. But historically, there have been few incentives for physicians to deliver evidence-based care. Compensation was not tied to the outcome of a hospital stay, or to educating or regularly monitoring patients with chronic disease. On the contrary, compensation in the fee-for-service (FFS) era encouraged episodic rather than continuous care. Today, we generally use the term pay for performance (P4P) to describe the financial incentives that are now in place to encourage physicians along a path of evidence-based medicine, prevention, and cost management. P4P emerged partly in response to counterproductive incentives created by FFS in the 1970s and 1980s and the backlash against the managed care that followed in the 1990s.

P4P, an outgrowth of utilization management review, began with quality performance measures and provider "report cards." What P4P typically means now is that providers are rewarded for meeting predetermined goals in the delivery of services. Although P4P has brought modest improvements in specific outcomes and increased efficiency, the general consensus is that P4P has not led to real cost savings, due to added administrative requirements. P4P also continues to stir controversy among providers as to the validity of what is being measured and rewarded. Meanwhile, such initiatives have not reached all physicians. Less than one-third of primary care physicians (PCP) in the United States reported any financial incentive for quality of care, according to a 2006 survey.[1]

Underlying most P4P programs is a laudable attempt to use clinical best practices as a driver of financial incentives. But we need to think strategically about how best to use these incentives as a tool for alignment. The majority of P4P programs to date have focused on what is easy to measure. These benchmarks fall largely in the areas of prevention and utilization, such as what percentage of patients receive flu shots or have mammograms on schedule. Another focus has been patient safety. This thrust is likely to continue, as a 2006 report from the Institute of Medicine called for incentives that aligned profitability with safety goals.[2]

Safety and preventive measures are important, of course. But if we really want to move the needle on improving patient health, we must use P4P to address the management and control of chronic diseases. I envision scenarios in which, rather than paying for performance, the goal will be to financially reward alignment. It may not be as complicated as it sounds. I envision programs that pay for participation in continuous disease management, with specific outcomes as a target. To get there, we may need to think simple and small in the beginning. For example, providers can be motivated to participate in activities that impact chronic disease control, such as ongoing disease management programs. Providers would receive pay-for-participation fees to enroll patients with chronic diseases in appropriate programs. They would get additional payments if patients achieve specific targets, and over time, provider incentive payments could become increasingly more outcomes based.

To this end, the most successful P4P programs will be:

- Multitiered

- Rich in actionable data

- Outcomes-based and focused on achieving a specific clinical goal, rather than a preventive step or a utilization measure

The concept of a multitiered P4P program is the most important of the three factors mentioned above. A multitiered P4P program has the following characteristics:

- Physicians are incentivized to spend sufficient time with patients so as to identify those with chronic disease.

- Providers are responsible for entering key patient information into a database.

- The physician and the payer agree on a detailed care plan. For example, consider patients with high blood pressure. The care plan for such patients might be quite specific, including requirements that the patient first take a diuretic and then an angiotensin-converting enzyme inhibitor if needed; that the patient reduce blood pressure to normotensive levels; and that the physician see the patient twice yearly. These goals, if met, are rewarded financially.

- Metrics are defined clearly, with specific targets agreed upon in advance. Achievement of clinical outcomes triggers payments. For each agreed-upon outcome—e.g., normal kidney function, blood pressure at 120/80, and so on—payment is made.

A Sampling of Economic Alignments

We are living in a time of runaway medical costs. The strategic goal of economic alignment is to maximize incentives that will lead to more cost-effective medical care. The tactics I describe are not intended to increase the profits of any one constituency; rather, they are to improve patient health and the delivery of care in a way that will keep the lid on escalating costs. There is no certain answer, no one-size-fits-all model to follow that will guarantee results in any particular market. Some programs leverage the carrot. Others leverage the stick. But to be successful, any pilot project must include the strategies that we have discussed: good data, transparency, and alignment.

One model I've touched on already involves paying for performance in connection with an outcome. Consider Dr. A, who wants to continue practicing as he always has, without incentives. Dr. B., on the other hand, accepts the health plan's option for higher compensation in exchange for more responsibility for disease management outcomes. Dr. B opts in for two specific areas of care: to putting every patient with hypertension on a beta-blocker and prescribing insulin for every diabetic patient who needs it. The payer continues to compensate Dr. A $50 per patient visit. But Dr. B will receive $70 per visit if he achieves the agreed-upon goals.

A variation on this scenario uses the stick instead of the carrot. That is, the payer asks providers to take responsibility for outcomes, but the provider bears more of the financial risk and the financial benefit. In this scenario, the payer might say to Drs. A and B that if patients with a history of myocardial infarction are not on a beta-blocker or a diabetic patient's blood sugar is not controlled, reimbursement for a patient visit will not be the usual $50 or the incentivized $70—but only $30.

In a second model of financial alignment—a variation on the shared savings model—the payer and provider target a specific percentage for improvement and work out the economics accordingly. For example, perhaps a plan's data shows that care for its diabetic patients is poor, with a high number of diabetic comas, amputations, and hospitalizations. The payer and provider (likely a large physician group or clinic) set a goal to improve outcomes by 20%, as evidenced by the payer's data. The payer and provider agree on how to measure that improvement, such as by tracking the number of hospital admissions for diabetic coma or the percentage of patients who complete interventions associated with diabetes control (monitoring hemoglobin A1c levels, achieving high prescription fill rates for diabetes medications, and so on).

If the target is reached, both clinically and financially, the payer and provider each receive half of the cost savings. If clinical goals are not reached, the provider does not receive his or her portion of the savings goal.

The alignment also could be worked out so that partial payments are available for partial success. The provider might receive a portion of the 10% savings in exchange for the extra work of identifying patients with chronic disease and another portion for putting such patients on a care plan. If providers meet the goals for caring for those patients, they receive their full 10% of the risk pool. Another option is simply to put the incentive payment on a scale: For whatever percentage of patients reach the clinical goals, the provider receives that percentage of his or her incentive payment.

A third model involves the provider taking on the total risk for a population, with the full potential reward. This is sometimes called the "global risk" model. Consider a 10-physician practice that sees 1,000 diabetic patients per year. An insurer studies the practice's data and finds those patients cost $1 million, with about $100,000 going to the physician practice. Hospitalizations cost $500,000, and another $400,000 goes to medications, radiology, and other services. The payer could offer to double the practice's compensation to $200,000 for managing those patients—with the goal that overall medical quality would improve primarily through better primary care, and that total annual costs for the patients would not exceed $800,000. Payer and provider would negotiate their responsibilities. (In Chapter 8, I'll address in more detail how these negotiations might include items such as whether the health plan would pay for a 1-800 number for patients or a care management program.)

We're beginning to see such arrangements around the country, especially in specialties that tend to work in large groups. For example, large cancer centers with 100 or more oncologists on staff are in some cases working within this global risk model. This is especially notable because of how difficult it is to reach clinical alignment around treating some cancers. Doctors may choose from multiple protocols involving many chemotherapeutic agents in a variety of combinations. Because some regions or physician groups prefer to use one protocol over others, clinical alignment on a broad scale is difficult. But when providers take on the global risk model, they can use the protocols they prefer without any questioning from the health plan because they are accepting responsibility for the results through their financial arrangement. In a global risk model, the role of health plans becomes focused on ensuring that high-quality medical care is indeed delivered. In practice, this means health plans monitor that care is delivered as was agreed upon with providers.

Every region and every market will have a configuration of economic alignment that best suits its physicians, hospitals, payers, and patient population. Ideas for economic alignment, when begun as pilot projects, will prove or disprove their worth for that community. And they will show potential to be duplicated else-where. The beauty of such experiments is that they can be executed relatively quickly, easily, and locally. They do not require a nationwide consensus, an over-haul of the health system, or elective politics. Thinking on a grand, national scale gets us bogged down in what cannot be done. I prefer to think on a smaller local or regional scale, as so many businesses do.

Economic alignments—formalized or not—abound in every community in nearly every industry. Consider the way realtors and car dealers interact, to the benefit of both. Car dealers keep tabs on real estate closings because they know that realtors may think about a new car after making a big sale. If the car dealer approaches the realtor with a promotion just at that time, each is likely to benefit. Simple tactics to align the benefits of two parties just makes good business sense.

Economic Alignment with Physician, Hospital, and Health Plan

Now that I've laid out some basic schematics for economic alignment, let's dig a little deeper into a potential alignment among physicians, a hospital, and a health plan.

In a hypothetical case, let's say that a health plan has figured out that 1,000 of its diabetic patients see a fairly small number of PCPs and consider a particular hospital to be "their hospital." This situation constitutes the geographic density that is ideal for a pilot project.

A closer look at physician records for the 1,000 diabetic patients shows that 50% are likely to have poor disease control based on underutilization of medical care and inadequate use of medications. The hospital data show a significant number of hospitalizations due to complications of uncontrolled diabetes among this group.

And the health plan's data show that these 1,000 diabetic patients cost $10 million per year.

To begin alignment, the three constituencies get together to look at these data and set their targets for improvement. They agree that physicians should increase compliance on insulin from 50% of eligible diabetic patients to 90%. Those patients also should control their hemoglobin A1c and receive yearly retinal scans. Such measures are likely to decrease emergency room visits and hospitalizations, so the parties agree on a goal of decreasing hospital utilization—emergency department and admissions combined—by 10%. The plan sets a goal of decreasing its costs for these diabetic patients by 3%, or $300,000.

Next, the three constituencies address specifics of their financial alignment. The plan offers PCPs, in exchange for the increased monitoring they will take on, half of the anticipated $300,000 cost reduction. Next, all three parties consider how they could better share information toward their common goal. (This falls into the all-important categories of connectivity and transparency.) To that end, the hospital commits to alerting the PCP, if possible, when a patient arrives in the emergency department. This practice could reduce hospital admissions, which is in the hospital's interest because inpatient stays for stabilizing the complications of chronic disease tend to not be profitable for the hospital.

With time, the hospital is likely to show a decrease in readmissions and inappropriate admissions. This is financially helpful to the hospital in the face of growing state refusals to pay for readmission within 30 days. A decrease in preventable admissions and readmissions could well prompt the payer to say, "I'll reimburse you a bit more because you are more effective than other hospitals."

It is not yet common for hospitals and insurers and physicians to come together and roll up their sleeves to work toward a mutually beneficial goal. But it is possible if someone just gets the process going.

Taking the scenario further, let's get into more detail about how the physician is paid and what he or she is paid for. Controlling chronic diseases—and the escalating costs associated with them—requires spending relatively small amounts up-front in the primary care setting to avoid expensive and high-intensity hospitalizations later.

Going back to our diabetic patients again, let's put together a theoretical model in which the insurer pays the PCP $100 for every patient visit. In the newly aligned program, the physician will be paid $105 for each diabetic patient visit—an extra $5 for simply identifying the patient as having diabetes and registering the patient as such with the insurer. The physician receives an additional $10 for putting the patient on a predesigned care map that payer and provider have agreed to. The physician receives an additional $15 if the patient maintains normal blood sugar levels and receives a retinal scan in the course of one year. Payments for maintaining normal blood sugar levels can be applied to periods between office visits as an ongoing incentive for the physician to work with the patient to maintain this level of disease control.

In aggregate, these payments can add substantially to the reimbursement of PCPs for taking steps that improve disease control and drive down medical costs through reduced utilization for high-cost events.

Now, let's put the patient into the equation. Let's say the patient had a copay of $25 for each visit. In our theoretical model, the patient, once registered, could be told that if he or she follows the care plan with this physician and participates in all of the follow-ups and preventive measures, the cost for all monitoring (such as kidney function tests and retinal scans) will be covered 100%. And, if the physician reports to the insurer that the patient's blood sugar is controlled, the patient's copay for each visit will drop from $25 to $10.

At first glance, many insurers would balk at the significant increases in payments to the PCP, while decreasing patient copays. But that would mean they are not looking at the big picture. For the extra primary care payments, the patient is receiving a lot more medical care. Let us assume that primary care payments increased by $100 per patient per year. Across the 1,000 diabetic patients in our theoretical model, the insurer would pay an extra $100,000 for primary care. Although this seems like a lot, we know, for example, that the financial effect of reducing hemoglobin A1c levels in diabetic patients by single percentage points can be profound. The added primary care costs could be recovered on a year-over-year basis through improvements in hemoglobin A1c levels and other measures and a resultant decrease in hospitalizations.

More importantly, the difference in medical costs between the well-controlled and poorly controlled diabetic populations would vary increasingly over time. The ramifications of uncontrolled disease are always likely to cost more than any extra payments supporting the continuum of care in a proactive way.

Outcomes and P4P

Interestingly, some insurers have struggled with the notion of P4P programs for providers. In their eyes, they have already been paying providers to deliver top performance. However, we now know that that philosophy has not delivered results.

One point worth emphasizing in regard to economic alignment and P4P is the significance of meeting the clinical target. Incentives should be paid only for reaching a clinical target, such as normal blood pressure or blood sugar levels. Progress in the direction of a clinical goal is just not the same as fully reaching that goal. If the constituents who are creating economic alignment feel it worthwhile to pay for a percentage of the patients reaching the target, that can be reasonable. Consider a clinical goal of achieving a blood sugar level below 115 mg/dl for 90% of diabetic patients. If 60% of patients achieve this level of blood sugar, it may be reasonable for the physician to receive two-thirds of the financial incentive. But incentives should not be paid for patients who do not reach the clinical goal. Evidence shows that blood sugar levels higher than 115 mg/dl cause damage to a patient's health.

Clinical outcomes that are clearly defined and an oversight process that ensures they are reached are essential to maintaining quality of care. In the early 1990s, there was strong public backlash against economic models that involved capitation—paying a physician a single fee for a patient, regardless of how many services the patient needed—due to issues that arose around the quality of care that patients under capitation received. Of the many ways to reduce costs, one is to deliver less care. This is why oversight around quality of care, outcomes measurement, and transparency around outcomes, are so important. Both sides—provider and payer—need to be clear as to the expectations for quality of care that must be delivered in any financial agreement outside of an FFS mechanism.

Using a carrot rather than a stick at the outset is a common strategy in seeking economic alignment, especially when encouraging adoption of technologies that ultimately will increase efficiency, patient safety, and quality of care. For example, Medicare is using a carrot that will turn into a stick to drive adoption of e-prescribing. Starting in 2009, physicians who use e-prescribing will receive a 2% increase in payments from Medicare. Five years later, physicians who still are not prescribing electronically will be penalized 2% of their payments.[3] Physicians who are rapid adopters of new technology may not need such incentives. But for physicians who are less keen on changing their habits, meaningful financial incentives may help move them forward.

Provider Scorecards as a Tool for Alignment

Physician scorecards are a tool for economic alignment when they are tied to physician compensation or to patient copayments. One interesting use is to address the different levels of service intensity employed by PCPs and specialists for some conditions that deliver the same clinical outcomes. It may be possible to align the financial incentives of the consumer and the physician in a way that encourages use of less costly options that have equal outcomes. Consider hypertension patients. A health plan could tell those patients that if they monitor their blood pressure and take medication regularly, the plan will lower their premium. To encourage patients to visit their PCP rather than a cardiologist, patients may be incentivized with lower copayments for primary care visits than for cardiologist visits. The plan benefits ultimately with fewer visits to the emergency department for chest pain.

The plan also could use a model in which physicians are paid an extra amount for certain outcomes of managing hypertension—such as patients not needing coronary angiograms or other expensive tests. This model might cause physicians to weigh more carefully the health benefits and risks of invasive tests. Instead, they might dedicate more resources to helping patients manage their conditions with appropriate medication and lifestyle management so that symptoms do not progress to the point of needing expensive diagnostic tests.

As a plan amasses data about how physicians manage heart disease, this information can be shared with patients. The data may affect patients' choice of providers and also be used as a tool of financial alignment. Perhaps the data will show that 98% of Dr. A's patients have their heart disease under control, as do 98% of Dr. K's patients. Yet the data might also show that 60% of Dr. A's patients undergo coronary angiograms versus only 10% of Dr. K's patients. Patients who prefer to avoid such invasive procedures might look at this data and choose Dr. K. The health plan, which prefers to avoid the cost of unnecessary testing, may increase its payment to Dr. K and let patients know his visits carry a lower copayment. The plan can go a step further and require a higher copayment for Dr. A, to further steer patient choice.

Although physician scorecards have been controversial, they are effective when based on good data. The data are most accepted by physicians when risk-adjusted, which levels the playing field for physicians whose patients are sicker to begin with.

It also is possible that financial incentives can be used to improve outcomes beyond the agreed-upon clinical goals. For example, it could be prenegotiated that physician payment for a hospitalized congestive heart failure patient is $600, with the stipulation that the patient remain hospitalized until goals are met for ejection fraction, fluids, and blood pressure. But if the patient is able to reach these goals in less than the five days expected, then the physician receives a financial incentive, as long as the patient is not readmitted within 30 days.

These examples all show that clinical alignment and financial alignment can be married successfully. The remaining questions are: How can providers collaborate with payers to meet their goals without being slowed down by bureaucracy, and how can they optimize their time and resources? The answer is administrative alignment.

ENDNOTES

1. Commonwealth Fund Slide #41 2006 Commonwealth Fund International Health Policy Survey of Primary Care Physicians (Schoen, et al., "On the Front Lines of Care," *Health Affairs* [November 2, 2006]), *www.commonwealthfund.org/publications/publications_show.htm?doc_id=419208* (accessed December 15, 2008).

2. Institute of Medicine (2006). "Preventing Medication Errors." The National Academies Press, 332, *http://books.nap.edu/openbook.php?isbn=0309101476&page=332* (accessed December 15, 2008).

3. Regina Herzlinger and Alfred Martin, *Connectivity in Healthcare* (Boston: Harvard Business School Press, 2008), 5.

Chapter 8
Achieving Administrative Alignment

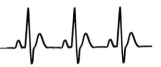

The word "administration" often carries a negative connotation in healthcare, especially because it so often is paired with the word "burden"—as in "administrative burden." We think of paperwork. We think of the back-and-forth phone calls, of lengthy forms to be filled out, of the fax machine spitting out denials or waiting for the next form we must send. I propose that we begin to think, instead, of creating administrative processes that aid in alignment and efficiency. Any system requires administration. *Good* administration can be used to improve quality and efficiency and lower costs. Administration can be a useful tool for the exchange of vital information between payers and providers.

But the reality we must deal with is that a large administrative burden exists today in the way healthcare is delivered and paid for in most settings. One of the great challenges we face is to achieve the clinical and economic alignment that is so necessary without adding to the administrative burden. This is especially true in trying to bring about clinical alignment. While the first and greatest challenge is achieving trust between payer and provider, the second is introducing administrative efficiency. How can we create a system that requires providers to interact with a set of rules, yet not burden them with a lot of bureaucracy? Even the most well-intentioned physician (or other provider) who agrees that prenegotiated clinical steps are medically appropriate will resist participating if the process is too burdensome or involves another layer of systems to log onto and forms to fill out. Clinical rules need to not only be sensible, but also well-integrated into the physician's work flow, particularly when it comes to performance measures and related metrics.

The general assessment to date is that, although pay-for-performance measures may have brought some improvements in outcomes and efficiency, potential cost savings mostly have been offset by increased administrative requirements. This is one of the reasons why adoption of technology solutions is so crucial in healthcare. If a payer and provider are using manual systems and another layer of manual processes is added for performance metrics, costs surely will go up. But if administrative processes are made more efficient—with electronic claims processing, portals to exchange information, and real-time conveyance of crucial patient data—true benefits can be realized.

Every physician would love to spend less time on the phone talking with health plans and more time on patient care. To embark on true care management, providers will need more sophisticated technologies than most currently have. It will be largely up to the plans to sponsor the introduction of technologies—as a way of showing willingness to invest in administrative efficiency that will lighten the provider's load and also increase transparency and data sharing.

Administrative ease is important to providers. Economic alignment does not come only in cash compensation to physicians and hospitals; payers' sponsorship of new technology for use in administrative services can certainly engage providers as well. This is where the clinical and economic aspects of their relationship come together. In the many examples of clinical and economic alignment in the prior two chapters, I described scenarios in which the cost of care decreases because providers are following evidence-based guidelines. It is reasonable that a portion of these savings be reinvested in administrative measures that will continue the trend toward more efficient healthcare.

When I think of administrative alignment, I consider all of the technology, services, infrastructure, and staff members that make it possible for providers to care for their patients and to get paid. But administration, to me, also means other services that extend patient care beyond the four walls of a hospital or clinic, such as social workers, 1-800 call lines, and patient education efforts.

When these services are connected to both the payer and provider, we create a feedback loop that sends useful information back to the provider. A provider that does not leverage all the tools available allows a big gap in the continuum of care. Without extended care and support for patients, the provider does not know what is going on once the patient steps outside the healthcare facility.

Let's take a look at some tools and scenarios for administrative alignment.

Why It Is Time to Retire the Fax Machine

Administrative alignment involves incentivizing providers to use technology, whether that means paying providers to use a technology, footing the bill for the technology itself, or some combination of the two. It is interesting to note that countries with a high degree of healthcare automation pay low percentages of their gross domestic product (GDP) on healthcare. Meanwhile, the United States continues to spend more of its GDP on healthcare than other countries, and yet has invested less in automation. The challenge is for payers and providers to collaborate on ways to use technology to reduce unnecessary spending.

An example of enormous waste in healthcare is the repeated re-creation of a patient's medical history. When a patient moves from the emergency department to an inpatient bed, the history may be taken all over again from scratch—usually from the patient's own recollection. Similarly, if a patient changes plans because an employer chose a new plan or because the patient changed jobs, the patient's history is lost completely. This is incomprehensible given modern technology, but all too true in the United States.

When a patient with a long history of chronic disease first enrolls in a new plan, that person appears to have no health problems, simply because no claims for that patient exist in that system. Creating a new history is time-consuming and costly, and the result is likely to be incomplete because it is based on the patient's recall. It will not contain specific lab values or test results. Although an electronic health record (EHR) with full interoperability is not currently available in every setting, it is worth a collaborative effort between payers and providers to bring one into play whenever possible.

The ability to perform transactions electronically is the most important technology for payer-provider administrative alignment. Auto-authorization means that a procedure is authorized using an automated system by the payer. A physician or hospital that regularly receives authorization for requested services on the first try—evidence that decision-making aligns with clinical evidence—can be rewarded with an expedited process for future authorization requests.

The payer can also dial up or down the intensity of auto-authorization. If a provider has a good track record for meeting performance metrics, less documentation typically will be required from that provider. For example, a plan could decide that a physician who has a 100% authorization rate for coronary angioplasty may, in the future, receive automatic approval when he requests the procedure—a great time and resource savings for his practice. However, a practice with a lower authorization rate may be required to provide more documentation, such as lab values, physician notes, and other relevant clinical data.

Electronic claims submission similarly could eliminate enormous amounts of personnel time for both payer and provider. To encourage its use, a provider could offer a financial incentive—perhaps a 5% increase in reimbursement for each claim submitted electronically versus manually. This is a simple step that could be incorporated into almost any pilot project.

The computerized claim processing known as auto-adjudication can also be used as an incentive. Whether the payer or provider initially funds the technology, both will be rewarded by the elimination of the cumbersome phone and fax processes that most claims processing still requires. Auto-adjudication is most useful if the computerized system shows an explanation as to why a claim is accepted or rejected. The response could note specifically whether medical evidence did or did not support use of a treatment for a patient, which would also aid the provider's future medical decision-making. This type of information feedback and transparency could move payers and providers toward greater clinical alignment. In the unaligned world, the health plan's decision-making process often seems like a black box to the provider. The provider knows only that a claim has been rejected and often continues to make the same mistakes that caused the rejection of the claim.

Ultimately, administrative alignment comes when both parties apply the same rules to medical decision-making and to payment. When a payer and provider first institute auto-authorization or auto-adjudication, neither would be applied across the board to all procedures. Rather, "the autos" are a tool that can be brought in, one procedure at a time, as payers and providers align in targeted areas. Alignment around these technologies is crucial. We should aim to retire, or at least use less of, the fax machine that has become a symbol of administrative burden and inefficiency.

But no technology will justify its investment if it is not fully leveraged. For example, in some facilities with e-prescribing capability, this technology is being used by only 30% of the health professionals who have access to it. If a provider has access to a portal with auto-adjudication, that provider's office staff must commit to using it and not fall back on old habits of phoning and faxing. Training may be necessary. Whoever is paying for the technology may want to introduce usage metrics as a condition of payment. For example, a payer might agree to pay for auto-authorization and auto-adjudication for a hospital's 200 physicians—but only if the hospital can show that the technology is being used for at least 95% of all eligible transactions.

Portals also are ideal for data-sharing. A payer portal for providers' use makes it possible for staff members to check on patient eligibility, benefit design, and patient copayments at the point of care. And portals can support efforts to implement auto-authorization and auto-adjudication, which are valuable tools for building payer-provider alignment. (Although a provider portal is optimal for the autos, it is possible to implement auto-authorization and auto-adjudication via telephony/interactive voice response.)

A portal also is extremely useful if it allows patient data to be shared among providers and between payers and providers. When a patient arrives at a hospital, time and resources are saved and unnecessary tests avoided if nurses there have access to a patient's history, medications, and prior testing. A portal also is ideal for reverse data-sharing, so that the plan will know the results of the patient's new tests. A nurse manager for the plan can flag those results to help the patient get needed services.

But even if you can't build a portal just now, you don't have to wait to begin collecting and exchanging data. Any information-gathering and sharing that gets information out of its traditional silos will help if the shared information is targeted and tactical. Sending real-time clinical data from a hospital to a health plan can assist with follow-up care and reduce readmissions. Pharmacy data—or more accurately, data that shows a prescription going unfilled—raises a red flag for the plan to reach out to the patient. Administrative systems such as these help complete a circle of care. The level of automation will increase the timeliness of the data and its usefulness.

Although a portal for patients that includes data from the plan and providers may be helpful, I do not regard this as the highest priority. The greatest utility of such information would be in maintaining an EHR—which ideally could be downloaded to physicians outside the plan if the patient changed plans.

A patient portal also could help enable Web visits between patient and provider. But Web visits are possible without a portal. Two of the largest commercial U.S. health plans already reimburse providers for Web visits, which can be time-efficient for the provider and the patient. Electronic prescription renewal is another great time-saver for physicians and can be tied in with safety systems, making it a cost-effective expenditure for payers.

Services, Infrastructure, and Personnel

When payer and providers seek to align, no action plan is complete without the payer asking the provider: What administrative processes do you have in place to make this work? Can we help? What would be most useful? This is where both payer and provider look carefully at their pain points. They should examine their data closely and zero in on services that would help fill gaps in the continuity of care. Then they must agree on who will provide the services and what information needs to be exchanged to bring about continuous, efficient care.

Potential services

For example, to reach a goal of medication compliance among diabetics, a plan might propose and pay for a 1-800 nurse call line for patients' questions or for disease management services. Whereas a physician may not have the skills or expertise to delve into patients' lifestyles or reasons for noncompliance with a plan of care, a payer and provider can agree to make sure patients receive other services to fill this gap. There are as many possible arrangements as there are pilot projects. One example, Medicare funds medical home demonstration projects. In addition to medical services, Medicare pays for relevant infrastructure and care coordination activities that the demonstration projects require.[1] Medicare shares with the medical practice a proportion of the amount by which expenditures are reduced as a result of a patient's enrollment in the trial, with the intent to deliver more outpatient care to control chronic disease and reduce high-cost medical care in a hospital setting.[2]

Optimize infrastructure

When payers and providers look at the services already in place, they need to consider whether they are working optimally. For example, too often, a 24-hour nurse line does not have adequate rules for what information should be conveyed to physicians. If physicians routinely receive reports full of unhelpful information, they will stop looking at those reports, and a valuable opportunity for intervention will be lost. To optimize the 1–800 nurse call line, a payer might offer to help pay for staff training or develop appropriate rules for triaging and escalating calls to the appropriate care provider.

Services that extend care beyond a provider's four walls may involve nurse counselors, social workers, behavioral specialists, and mental health professionals. These professionals can stratify patients in many ways: by the severity of their conditions, comorbidities, financial issues, compliance, and need for education. A patient who is hospitalized due to a complication from diabetes, but is knowledgeable about her disease and compliant, may be assigned to receive a phone call from a nurse manager only every other week. Another patient who has much more difficulty adhering to a medication regimen may instead be assigned to receive calls at home more frequently, be provided with more education, or be issued a home monitoring device.

A care team might involve a nurse, a social worker, and a pharmacist. A social worker has the time, training, and methods to find out, for example, if patients cannot afford their medications and direct them to a program for financial assistance. A pharmacist, as part of a care team, educates patients about their medications and can assist with financial and pharmacy assistance program enrollments.

Of the parties involved, a payer is most likely to have the resources to pay for such support services. However, a patient is more likely to engage with the services if they are offered through a physician's office, because patients tend to trust their doctors more than they trust their payers. Communication of a patient's needs back to the insurer will help drive the resources where needed to complete a patient's care.

Extended care and support mechanisms and services need to be part of a provider's tool set, as they can help the provider know whether a patient is complying with the regimen prescribed.

One example that weds technology with extended care and administrative alignment is home monitoring. A patient with high blood pressure can be given a home monitoring device in which he checks his blood pressure twice daily, or a diabetic can use a system to check his or her blood sugar. Home monitoring might be ideal for a patient who repeatedly lands in the hospital because she has difficulty complying with her diabetes medications.

Home monitoring devices are relatively inexpensive and require only brief participation by patients. Patients' data travels via a phone modem to a nurse manager, who keeps an eye out daily for whether patients' conditions are well-controlled. When necessary, a physician can be alerted if the biometric studies are showing uncontrolled blood pressure or blood sugar, and intervention can be initiated. This is the kind of loop that completes care and can bring patients back into the primary care setting for additional care or services before their conditions deteriorate.

Place appropriate personnel

Assigning appropriate staff members and resources to a project must be part of the initial planning. When budgets are tight, case managers and similar social services providers traditionally are seen as nonrevenue-producing and, therefore, are the first to be cut. But doing so is shortsighted.

Keep in mind that many of these roles can be outsourced as well. More important is that everyone interacting with a patient is part of the continuity of care and that the information they gather is integrated with the patient data of the payer and provider. Support services providers are contributing to keeping the patient healthy and keeping costs down. If the financial alignment is such that the provider is taking on the full financial risk for the medical needs of patients, the payer might agree to pay the full cost of extra nurses or case managers to address barriers to care for the patient. Or the payer and provider could agree on the services needed and what it would cost, with the payer providing the services at a monthly fee per patient, charged back to the provider. If a provider already has staff members in place, the alignment can come via the payer offering staff members additional training.

As more physicians become employees of hospitals, with fixed salaries, the administrative alignment that a payer can offer will be an important incentive. Although some providers cringe at what appears to be extra work to gather data on patients and outcomes, automation can vastly simplify the process by reducing the time that all staff members spend on back-and-forth calls and faxes with payers. Removing the burden of administration allows clinicians to spend more time providing care.

ENDNOTES

1. John K. Iglehart, "No Place Like Home," *New England Journal of Medicine,* 359 (12): 1200–1202 *http://content.nejm.org/cgi/content/full/359/12/1200* (accessed December 13, 2008).

2. John K. Iglehart, "No Place Like Home," *New England Journal of Medicine,* 359 (12): 1200–1202 *http://content.nejm.org/cgi/content/full/359/12/1200* (accessed December 13, 2008).

Chapter 9
A Model for Care in Pennsylvania

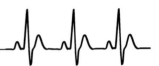

A few years into the new millennium, health officials for the state of Pennsylvania sought to improve healthcare for their rural Medicaid population. The capitated managed care model that was being used in the state's urban and suburban areas wasn't quite right for rural areas. In addition to the usual needs of a Medicaid population, the state's challenges with providers were plentiful: Pennsylvania's Medicaid reimbursement was traditionally very low, rural specialists were in short supply, and a recent conversion of the state's claims processing system had left providers feeling frustrated.

These are the types of real-world challenges that many of us in healthcare face every day. It can be difficult to address the individual needs and quirks of particular markets and locales.

Pennsylvania responded to its own needs with the ACCESS Plus program, which illustrates many of the principles I've described throughout this book. Does the program leverage to the maximum degree every tool available today? No, it does not. No single program can push every lever, optimize every technology, and address all circumstances and issues.

However, the Pennsylvania program does include crucial elements of clinical, economic, and administrative alignment. It reflects the needs and resources of the region. It keeps caregivers and patients at the center. And, it shows how collaboration and transparency can be applied to a real-world situation. The ACCESS Plus program, despite limitations, has improved health outcomes, reduced costs, and achieved a high level of satisfaction among providers and patients in rural Pennsylvania. Here is the story of ACCESS Plus.

The ACCESS Plus Story

In 2003, Pennsylvania's top health officials set out to devise a new model of fee-for-service (FFS) managed care for the Medicaid population in the state's 42 rural counties. They wanted to expand an existing primary care case management (PCCM) program for children to extend services to adults, focus on care management rather than cost, and introduce a performance-based program for physicians. The state's main goals were to improve the quality of clinical care and provide enhanced care coordination.

By summer 2004, a request for proposal (RFP) was developed for an outside vendor to manage the program, now known as ACCESS Plus, for 280,000 children and adults in the FFS rural market in Pennsylvania. The vendor was to create pathways between the consumers, the payer (the state), and the providers, with the goal of improving the population's health status. In early 2005, the contract was awarded to McKesson Health Solutions. The program would continue to pay providers in the FFS manner, but with the addition of case management and disease management functions for participating patients, as is more typical in managed care delivery systems. Key points of the program called for:

- Integration of PCCM and disease management by the contractor

- A network of primary care physicians (PCP) maintained by the contractor, with establishment of medical homes for enrollees

- Use of predictive modeling to assist with high-risk case identification and to establish a referral process to disease management and intense case management

- Coordination between behavioral and physical health entities

- Disease management for asthma, diabetes, congestive heart failure (CHF), chronic obstructive pulmonary disease, and coronary artery disease (CAD)

- Provider and enrollee call centers

- Establishment of quality measures

- A provider pay-for-performance (P4P) program

While the vendor took on medical management functions, the state continued to be responsible for enrolling patients and providers, paying providers, prior authorizations for services, and performing utilization management.

Earlier in this book, I described the ideal area for a pilot project as a single region with a concentration of payers, providers, and/or patients. The rural Pennsylvania market did not meet those criteria exactly. But it did have the advantage of being all within one state, with a sole payer (Pennsylvania Medicaid), and goals that were highly focused.

The project also varied from the ideal in that it began with almost no clinical metrics to use for an initial analysis. Very little data had been collected as to how the state's rural physicians were practicing. However, there were abundant claims data available. In fact, the state provided two years of claims data at the member level for all responders to the RFP. The state had a robust quality and clinical reporting program, HealthChoices, in place for its managed care programs, and one goal of the ACCESS Plus project was to create a similar system that would emulate HealthChoices.

James Hardy, former project manager for FFS operations and policy and former deputy secretary of the Office of Medical Assistance Programs in the Pennsylvania Department of Public Welfare, was one of the leaders of the project. Hardy helped develop and implement the ACCESS Plus program. He stated that the initial act of creating the proposal for the program brought a clearer understanding of the region's needs, what the existing system of care was lacking, and what the program's goals should be.

From the start, one great asset for ACCESS Plus was support from the very top of state government. Improving care for Medicaid patients in rural areas was one of the four pillars of a strategic plan that already had been approved by the state administration, with sign-off all the way up to the governor's office.

As part of the budget process, consensus around the goal of improving care for rural Medicaid patients came quickly, including in the state legislature. In seeking legislative approval, state health officials worked extensively with providers and community health advocates to reach consensus on the idea of extended care management within the FFS system.

Many rural physicians had negative feelings about managed care, so they were pleased with the alternative offered through ACCESS Plus. It took just three or four months, Hardy said, for all the necessary stakeholders to agree that the program should go forward.

It was a given, from the start, that the care management aspect of the program would be outsourced. With budget constraints and a political imperative not to expand state government, outsourcing the project was the most politically viable way to experiment. If the program didn't work, it could easily be brought to an end.

Governance for ACCESS Plus began with a quality management committee (QMC) that was responsible for policy and guideline approval, review of key clinical quality indicators, and oversight of teams and work groups that reported to the committee quarterly. The QMC included both external members (provider representatives, enrollees, and associated contractors) and internal members (medical directors from the Department of Public Welfare and other department staff members), with and without voting rights. It also included representation from McKesson, as the contractor responsible for disease management and the overseer of a subcontractor that continued the existing PCCM program. This committee reviewed survey results, medical record audit results, complaints, and backlog reports.

Significantly, the QMC had oversight of the program's main operational entity, the ACCESS Plus quality improvement committee, which met bimonthly. Membership comprised internal members from the welfare department, McKesson, and the subcontractor responsible for the PCCM program. Hardy served as the team lead (see Chapter 3 for more about this role). At any given time, he was aware of all-important issues with the program and could respond to any stakeholder, at any level, about its progress. Reporting to Hardy was a strong leader with responsibility for day-to-day operations.

Clinical and economic alignment

From the outset, a goal of the program was to generate clinical alignment where possible. Because so little quality-related data existed about the population and medical practices in the region, the state needed to first start gathering the data. This was not ideal, as data analysis ideally is the foundation of designing a program. But the state's organizers realized that they couldn't let this impede them from moving forward with a program that ultimately would gather the necessary information.

The clinical outcomes used to align the payer and the providers for the ACCESS Plus program were basic enough that there was little dispute. Initially, the clinical alignment came primarily from providers endorsing the program, providing enrollee contact information to the contractor, and encouraging their involvement in disease management programs. The alignment also came through prescribing appropriate medications based on clinical practice guidelines in conjunction with the state's preferred drug list.

As the program was being designed, simply getting patients into the care process and engaging both payers and providers in care management was a goal that drove both clinical and economic alignment. But ultimately, the program's architects sought to create a medical home model that would incentivize physicians to see patients more frequently, to help manage their care better, and to help consumers change their behaviors.

Recruiting physicians to participate in a Medicaid program was one of the biggest challenges. Medicaid payments in Pennsylvania historically were very low—just 40% of what Medicare typically pays for a similar service. Increasing the payment for a patient visit by a small amount—from $25 to $27 per patient visit, for example—would not be enough motivation for physicians to take on Medicaid patients.

Instead, the program aimed to engage PCPs with a financial reward just for saying they would participate. One underlying principle of the program's design was that providers would see those rewards rapidly.

Repeatedly, Hardy heard from reluctant physicians: "You're going to ask us to do something new, but you aren't going to pay us." There was great concern that this sentiment would be a strong barrier to physician participation. And it may well have been why physicians moved into the P4P program slowly.

State officials felt that a pay-for-*participation* incentive was crucial, and it was decided that physicians would receive $200 for simply agreeing to participate in the ACCESS P4P program. Physicians could also earn $30 per patient for encouraging that patient to participate in the program and providing the contractor with the patient's contact information. Identifying a high-risk patient who was a candidate for disease management paid an additional $40 per patient.

The pain point for the state was uncontrolled chronic disease in this rural Medicaid population. Too often, a patient with chronic disease went unidentified or received little to no care until a crisis sent him or her to the emergency room, usually after significant disease progression. A guiding principle behind the financial incentives of ACCESS Plus was to reward providers—and to do so quickly—for helping to draw patients into the program, identify those with chronic disease, and address the diseases.

The second phase of the program rollout was "payment for collaboration." Physicians were eligible for a $60 payment, twice yearly per patient, for putting a patient on a care plan and documenting this plan in a chronic care feedback form used by disease management nurses employed by McKesson.

Incentives in the third phase were paid for patient use of key medications for four target conditions: CHF, diabetes, asthma, and CAD. In the first year, use of medications was based on the patient's self-report via a telephone assessment. In the second year, claims data and lab reports were used to reward physicians for measurement of low-density lipoprotein (LDL) cholesterol for diabetes and for patient use of beta-blockers for CHF, statins for CAD, and a controller medication for asthma. Physicians could receive $17 per patient each year for medication compliance, and were eligible for multiple payments if that patient had several conditions that were measured.

Participating in ACCESS Plus could earn a physician $200 more per high-risk patient than was possible under the prior FFS program. ACCESS Plus was designed to steer money to the providers most actively engaged with the complex and costly patients. This approach was very different from the alternative of simply increasing reimbursement for any and all primary care office visits.

Because of physicians' initial skepticism, the P4P compensation was documented with great transparency and is publicly available at *www.accessplus.org*. This was a natural outgrowth of Pennsylvania's long-standing transparency in regard to Medicaid policies, Hardy noted. In my view, this degree of transparency should be a goal of every project. When providers see compensation outlined explicitly, it builds trust. Also, in many markets, there is large variation in compensation. For providers, the knowledge that they will be paid the same amount for the same service as every other provider also builds trust. This is a huge stepping-stone toward alignment.

In its second year, ACCESS Plus was enhanced to include incentives for adherence to best practice guidelines for the management of chronic disease, pediatric measures, and greater focus on women's health. This reflects the constant evolution of programs. Achievements can be realized, but they may be accomplished incrementally. Buy-in and transformation are processes that require time, a road map, education, and conditioning. Pennsylvania has achieved care management changes that would not have been possible at the get-go. This project is proof positive that successful change is often incremental.

Administrative alignment

One goal of the ACCESS Plus project, and particularly the role of the outside vendor, was to move beyond the payer-provider antipathy that had developed over the years. Low Medicaid reimbursements in particular were a source of contention. State officials wanted the provider relationship to focus on the medical care that patients receive rather than the cost of care. The state consciously wanted to create a clean split administratively between providing care and paying for it. Part of McKesson's role was to create positive patient encounters with physicians by providing guidance for care management. The state, meanwhile, would handle the business relationship and continue in the traditional payer role of resolving payment and eligibility issues.

ACCESS Plus, through its partnership with McKesson, deployed many of the administrative tools I've discussed previously to support physicians and patients, including call center creation, disease management, and intense medical case management, and the addition of healthcare employees throughout the community. In the face of pressures not to expand state government, outsourcing care management was a means to address needs and measure results on a trial basis.

Among the administrative innovations was a paperless referral process. In recent years, the industry has moved away from requiring referrals to see specialists. Patients dislike having to get referrals, and the use of paper for referrals seems archaic. Yet referrals were an intentional component of ACCESS Plus, meant to cement the relationship between the patient and the PCP, who was to be the driver of each patient's care. To achieve the desired behavior with as little administrative burden as possible, the program's leaders came up with a paperless process. The specialist simply had to enter the PCP's number into a referral box on the claim, and the state would pay. The process was not as robust or rigid as the traditional referral process. However, this minimal exchange of information achieved the goal of reinforcing the relationship between the PCP and the specialist—and of reinforcing the medical home concept with the patient.

Surprisingly, even before the policy went into effect—that is, after the state announced the policy, but before it began refusing claims that lacked the PCP number—physicians started adhering to it. Just announcing the change, and making it as easy as possible, had the sentinel effect. Primary care visits were on the rise.

The Pennsylvania program could not take advantage of all of today's technological advances, given the Medicaid program's technology at the outset and the limited state budget. There were limited auto-authorization and auto-adjudication processes and no electronic health records or portals. But ACCESS Plus did leverage what was available. It made the most of its history of transparency with physicians and built on an existing PCCM program. The program, while ambitious for state government, was realistic in the scope of what it could accomplish in its initial phases and focused on taking steps that would be measurable and could be built upon later.

The results

In the first year of the program, emergency room use decreased from 61.1% per 1,000 member months in 2005 to 55.4% in 2006. This seemed directly attributable to the improved care coordination that was a key aspect of the program's medical home concept.

Another measure of success: ACCESS Plus significantly exceeded the 2006 and 2007 national Healthcare Effectiveness Data and Information Set (HEDIS®)[1] averages for PCP and dental visits. Among the 37,000 participants in disease management programs during the first year, ACCESS Plus assessed this population using HEDIS-like data collection methods and concluded:

- Poorly controlled hemoglobin A1c decreased from 43.3% to 35.5% among diabetes patients

- Cholesterol management in diabetes patients (LDL < 100) increased from 25.3% to 31.8%

- Persistence of beta-blocker usage in people with CAD increased from 55.8% to 67.9%

- Appropriate use of asthma controller medications in asthma patients increased from 79.4% to 87.5%

One aim of ACCESS Plus was that "we wanted the value that would come from managing the consumers rather than managing the costs," Hardy said. But in managing patient care, costs went down. In the program's first year, net savings compared to projected costs were $27 million for the disease management population. In the second year, net savings grew to $35.9 million.

The program was recognized as one of 15 finalists for the 2008 Innovations in American Government Award from the Ash Institute for Democratic Governance and Innovation at Harvard Kennedy School. This awards program was designed to improve government practice by honoring effective government initiatives and encouraging the dissemination of such best practices nationwide. In addition, the program also received the 2008 Outstanding Provider Engagement Initiative Award from DMAA: The Care Continuum Alliance.

Although ACCESS Plus did not employ a full provider-driven model, it was a model that worked with the local realities and resources available. Let's put it in the context of the example that I have used frequently regarding variations in the treatment of prostate disease: If the only provider who treats prostate disease in a rural area is a urologist, it is no use for a payer to say it will reimburse only for treatment done by radiation oncologists.

In hindsight, we see that ACCESS Plus might have been more successful at drawing providers into the program faster if more money had been allotted for P4P measures in addition to rewarding for program participation. But as one of the first Medicaid programs with a P4P component, this was new ground. Over-coming the mistrust that had developed between payers and providers was one of the biggest obstacles. Provider participation rates in ACCESS Plus have continued to rise. P4P measures have expanded, and more money has been allocated for them. With the approach working, the state has been willing to invest more in P4P, based on measurable results.

Success came, ultimately, because the provider community felt heard. The capitated managed care model used for Medicaid patients in other parts of the state was not a good fit for the rural areas. And conventional thinking about competitive pricing and the value of competition was not effective in a rural area in which competition was minimal, because all patients went to the same providers. Physicians appreciated that the state created an alternative to the managed care model. A provider survey showed a high level of satisfaction with the program, and feedback from the survey was used to guide subsequent program improvements.

Rewards will come, in clinical and financial results, when payers focus on the physicians who are most actively engaged with the patients whose needs are greatest. Payers must work with these physicians to align around clinical care that is evidence-based and physician-directed, with concurrent economic and administrative alignment. The initial levers to push may vary region by region. But physician empowerment, coupled with the right physician incentives, will work in every market and in every circumstance.

ENDNOTE

1. HEDIS® is a registered trademark of the National Committee for Quality Assurance.

Chapter 10
The Future for Payers and Providers

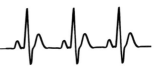

We face serious challenges in healthcare in the rapidly arriving future. Looking squarely at the facts, it is clear that our current healthcare system is standing on a burning platform. Consider the following:

- Patients are getting older, getting healthier, and staying alive longer. This is good news for individual patients. For the healthcare system, it means addressing an over-65 population that will double by 2030.

- Serious diseases such as HIV and many forms of cancer are becoming chronic diseases that patients live with. Again, this is good news for patients. But the healthcare system will potentially need to care for these patients for decades.

- Between 20% and 70% of people with chronic illness in the United States have not yet been identified by the healthcare system. As healthcare becomes more efficient, we will be able to identify many more of these patients—and will need to treat them for extended periods of time.

These three factors add up to a need for more healthcare occurring in the primary care setting and more primary care physicians (PCP). However, there is now a physician shortage, especially in primary care, and it is projected to get worse.

If we do nothing to alter our present course, the healthcare system is poised for meltdown, probably by 2020 or sooner. Demand for primary care will surge as supply dwindles. This imbalance will lead to even more patients using the emergency department for primary care, which will likely balloon to a problem of enormous financial proportions.

The solution, which needs to begin immediately, will not come through sweeping nationwide change, but by experimenting with aligned models at the local level, measuring the results to learn what works best, and recreating similar programs elsewhere.

The United States spends 16% of its gross domestic product (GDP) on healthcare—far more than many countries that produce better health outcomes.[1] The U.S. mortality rate is 110 deaths per 100,000 people, while Japan—which spends just 8% of its GDP on healthcare—has a mortality rate of 71 per 100,000 people.[2]

One common thread worldwide is that countries with the lowest spending and best results also have the highest rate of technology adoption. The Commonwealth Fund has noted that 28% of U.S. physicians used electronic medical records (EMR) in 2006.[3] By contrast, 98% of physicians in the Netherlands used EMRs in 2006; that country spent just 9% of GDP on healthcare (in 2004) and had a mortality rate of 82 per 100,000 (2002–2003). New Zealand, with 92% of physicians using an EMR system, spent 8% of GDP on healthcare. Perhaps most striking is Singapore, which has great outcomes with just 3% of its GDP devoted to healthcare. The healthcare system there is highly automated. It is clear that technologies that involve all the major parties in healthcare are essential to reducing waste and to increasing alignment.

When I travel abroad, health experts in countries with the most successful healthcare profiles pinpoint two areas in which the United States has gone off track. "You didn't embrace technology," is the first comment I tend to hear. My counterparts abroad are incredulous that we still use paper systems at all. In some countries, such as Denmark, the degree of alignment and technology allows auto-adjudication to be the default; claims have been virtually eliminated.

The second comment concerns the role of the physician: "You took the provider out of the equation." Indeed, we have created parallel processes around the physician, such as traditional disease management initiatives. As we look to the future, it is crucial that we leverage the physician and technology.

Leveraging the Provider

Leveraging our providers is the key to the future. This means putting the physician at the center of care and equipping the physician with the tools to effectively manage patients and outcomes. The concept of the medical home—a term I fear could be worn out without fulfilling its promise—warrants discussion here. I prefer to use the expanded concept of the "patient-centered, provider-guided medical home."

In this model, a PCP (or group) knows each patient's medical history, provides primary care, and is the first stop when a medical need arises. The medical home provider refers patients to additional resources—be it a surgeon, a social worker, or a disease management program. A medical home, at its best, is an expression of payer-provider connectivity, with the physician at the center of care.

To succeed, the medical home needs economic alignment to incentivize physicians toward managing outcomes across the continuum of a patient's health. It needs administrative alignment in the form of staff members to coordinate care and an infrastructure to support them. And it needs data and a sophisticated database that can capture the information that will be used to manage patients. Without these elements, care arrangements may function similarly to the old gatekeeper model—even if they are called "medical homes."

Fully leveraging the provider means all providers. The alignments that have been the focus of this book—clinical, economic, and administrative—must involve all professionals who provide care, including nurses, physician assistants, pharmacists, social workers, case managers, and others. Their contributions will be optimized if they are aligned. Aligning all providers makes the best use of the most costly resources, including the physician's time. Reducing what physicians regard as "the hassle factor" that accompanies modern medicine goes a long way toward alignment.

As we face expanding primary health needs, "minute clinics" and retail medicine offer a potential pressure valve to relieve some of the burden on the primary care system. But these new clinics will be effective only if they are connected and aligned with the rest of the healthcare system. A retail clinic that exchanges data with a patient's payer and PCP is useful to all parties.

The trend toward physician employment by hospital systems has many implications for alignment—one of which is a trend toward increased use of technology. Cost has been a barrier for small physician groups to add electronic records and other types of automation to their practices. As more practices become owned by hospital systems, the hospital systems will put a lot of their technological infrastructure into those practices to create a sort of technology ecosystem. Doing so holds the promise of greater administrative efficiency and fewer wasteful errors. This also will create connectivity among providers that could enhance clinical alignment.

Let's think back to the cardiologist who responds to a patient's chest pain with a cardiac catheterization instead of a less costly and invasive echocardiogram, which is equally effective as a diagnostic. Preserving physician autonomy—while reducing unnecessary and expensive tests that fall outside evidence-based medicine (EBM)— is a huge challenge. Physician employment in hospital systems likely will decrease the variation in practice patterns within a region, as these physicians may be more likely to follow the evidence-based guidelines of the hospital.

Integration of specialists and PCPs within a hospital system also may create internal incentives for specialists to practice more cost-effective medicine. Hospital systems that own both specialty and primary care practices increasingly are asking large insurers or employers for higher reimbursements in exchange for better management of patient care, which is possible because of the clinical alignment under their roof. Their doctors are saying, in effect: "We are going to be so judicious among our own physicians that we're going to deliver very high-quality care, and we're going to strive to minimize excessive testing and duplication. And if we save a lot of money, we should keep a lot of money." Within this global risk model, the providers are aligned. For every unnecessary catheterization that is avoided, the whole system is able to see additional profits.

Whatever changes the future brings, the fundamental payer-provider dynamics will continue to exist. And so will the need for payers and providers to align. Openness, transparency, and collaboration will be key. Accountability must be built into every reimbursement model to keep collaboration strong. Clinical alignment, in which payer and provider agree on definitions, best practices, and measurable outcomes, will be the cornerstone.

As we discuss keeping the physician at the center of care, let's not overlook the role of the physician executive, which should be cultivated. Business-minded and collaborative physicians are valuable in leadership positions. The physician executive understands what is involved in day-to-day patient care, understands how physicians think, and can help bridge the gap between payers and providers.

Leveraging Technology

My optimism for our future stems, in part, from the enormous promise of technology. The ability to gather, share, analyze, and model data will bring us into a new era, if we choose to use it. But who will pay for the technology? For now, I believe it is the responsibility of the payers. They have the resources, scale, and potential to gain the most from the efficiencies of technology. If a new technology improves outcomes in both cost and quality, payers will see a very high return on their investment.

Hospital systems and large, multidisciplinary practices also have the economic wherewithal to fund technology innovation. Too often, though, I see providers add new technologies and trumpet them as a marketing tool. This alone will not bring value. Using technology to its fullest to lower the cost and improve the quality of care is what brings the greatest return on investment. A provider that effectively leverages automation is in a good position to seek increased reimbursements from payers for the increased efficiency and accuracy that automation can bring. I do want to acknowledge that implementing technology is a time-consuming endeavor that requires perseverance and a willingness to learn. But, the rewards are there for those who carry it through.

Financial incentives for automation are growing. For example, Medicare is planning to increase payments for providers who use e-prescribing. This is a win-win for all parties, because everyone benefits from automated prescribing and fewer adverse events.

In the years ahead, might one of the technology giants enter the arena and build a hugely data-rich system as its contribution to healthcare? Might the financial services industry, with a track record for creating connectivity and an interest in the transactional side of healthcare, offer a solution? We don't know the answer yet. But for now, payers are in the best position to introduce automation. The financial side of healthcare has been automating more quickly than the clinical side. The desire to get paid quickly and accurately has driven providers toward electronic bill submission and the technologies around it. But the technology for clinical alignment has been adopted much more slowly.

Among the reasons for slow adoption of clinical decision-making tools in the United States is that physicians simply prefer to rely on their own knowledge and experience, which they can access more quickly than turning to a computer. But as the wealth of information escalates, no one will be able to continue to process it all.

Increasingly, technology will have to play a role in medical decision-making. Research has shown that the typical human brain can incorporate up to about 10 variables when making a decision. But exploding knowledge in healthcare, particularly findings regarding the human genome, will quickly outstrip the ability of even the smartest individuals to make decisions that take all available variables into consideration. Each day, discoveries tell us more about the genetic markers that are associated with disease. We also are learning how genetic variants may be linked to the effectiveness of a particular therapeutic. Prior to this knowledge, doctors looked only to family history for clues about a patient's genetic makeup.

It is now projected that by the year 2014, we will have identified at least 100 genomic markers that are known variables in how to treat an individual's hypertension. Even the most attentive physician will not be able to keep up. With more genomic variables being understood each month, by the year 2025, there will likely be as many as a 1,000 variables affecting any medical decision. Decision-making tools available in the near future will be able to determine which drugs, based on an individual's genetic profile and known variables, will be most effective. The amount of clinical data simply is exceeding the ability of that marvelous information-processing system—the human brain—that to date has served medicine so well.

What We've Learned and Where It Will Take Us

Even the least successful experiments and experiences in healthcare during the past 20 years have provided vital information about what works. We know that components of a successful healthcare model must include better technology, better data integration, and more sharing of data. We have learned the importance of information, in its many forms, to each constituency. We know now that patient behavior and behavior modification are critical to managing illness. We have seen the value of pay for performance as a tool that we can further refine.

As the scenarios presented in this book show, the successful model of healthcare in the future is likely to involve a true partnership and information-sharing between the payer and provider. Within a particular geographic area, this begins with a historical look at claims and other data for a category of patients. The payer and provider then agree on a treatment plan and measurable goals for this patient group. The plan design gives physicians incentives to spend the time needed with patients to achieve the desired outcome. If a physician group does not have the infrastructure or nursing staff to provide the necessary behavior modification for a patient, the payer should help fill those gaps. The payer and provider work together toward a common goal—which can be as simple as driving a patient's blood sugar level below 115 mg/dl and keeping it there. This is a viable model that will bring results.

Role of consumer

I have focused primarily on the payer-provider relationship in this book and have kept consumers and employers at the periphery of the discussion. However, both groups obviously have a role to play in alignment.

It is the consumer's responsibility to make good choices about health and the financial aspect of paying for healthcare. Patients must understand the importance of a healthy lifestyle and act on that information, especially as it pertains to a medical condition. It is the patient's responsibility to understand his or her own treatment plan and to ask questions until it is clear. The patient must know which further evaluations and provider visits are needed and follow through.

Meanwhile, the provider and payer must act as the principal parties responsible for supplying this information to patients. Delivering the right information at the right time and in the right form, and supporting consumers through any issues or concerns are important goals of payer-provider alignment.

Bringing patient decision-making into alignment may require financial incentives for the patient. Incentives could be offered for behavioral goals, medication adherence, and recommended follow-up visits and tests. A diabetes patient who does not control his or her blood sugar levels, or a smoker who continues the habit, might face higher copays. Or, a financial incentive could be offered for maintaining healthy blood sugar and achieving smoking cessation.

Consumer-directed products will help introduce efficiencies only if patients have adequate information, tools, and transparency to help them make decisions.

For consumer-directed products to work, a diabetes patient must have the information and incentive to seek out medical care when it is indicated, as well as access to physicians who have the best track records for delivering the needed care.

Role of employers

Employers, as the architects of benefit design, can function as a primary impetus of change. In their individual and collective endeavors, employers deserve credit for some of the best innovations and trends in recent years. They have forced a lot of positive changes. Employers have championed the medical home model and transparency in provider performance information. Employers should continue pushing for incentives for both providers and patients to make the choices that lead to high-quality, cost-efficient care. Employers could insist on including the following four elements in plan designs to improve transparency across all constituencies:

- **Provider transparency.** Provider information on outcomes should be as transparent to patients as possible so they can make informed decisions around provider selection. For example, a patient facing coronary artery bypass graft surgery should be able to find out how many such procedures have been done by each doctor in his area or in his plan, the outcomes, and the rate of complications.

- **Physician empowerment and incentives.** Delivering medical care that will lead toward desired outcomes in a cost-effective manner should be rewarded with incentives.

- **Patient incentives.** If a patient adheres to a care plan, he or she should be rewarded with lower copays or other costs.

- **Employee reports.** These reports would quantify how employees, in the aggregate, are doing. An employer would be able to find out how many of their employees have chronic conditions such as diabetes and, of those, what percentage are controlled or not controlled.

A comprehensive approach to benefit design would include all of these interrelated elements. Clinical alignment cannot be achieved unless providers see the value of their extra time and work and are compensated; transparency won't be achieved without incentives.

Many Interdependencies, But No Big Fix

Rather than rolling out a big nationwide plan with one dynamic, employers and insurers will achieve more with a smaller regional plan that includes the multiple, interdependent dynamics required for success. An employer could say it wants transparency for all providers across an entire employee base of 40,000 people. But that approach will not be as effective as focusing on a single geographic area. In a concentrated location, a payer can incentivize physicians to use care plans, EBM, and transparency. Putting three to four interdependencies in a local area will drive results more effectively than trying to spread a blanket of transparency far and wide. The greatest value lies in getting a critical mass of interdependencies together so that you see results. The sum of the parts in a concentrated region is greater than one component applied in a larger area.

Unfortunately, we too often have tried to apply a one-pronged strategy across a wide swath of the market. An example is the recent surge in consumer-directed products. The concept may be good. But do plans offering such products provide patients with the information on provider cost, quality, and outcomes needed to make informed choices? Are patients educated about their diseases in ways that will help them manage their health better? Do they have the necessary tools, such as a health calculator or an electronic patient record, to track their progress? Can they communicate easily with their physician, perhaps through an e-visit?

Interdependent initiatives require more complex planning. This is why account-ability mapping—stating clearly and precisely who is responsible for each piece of a plan—is so crucial.

Payer and Provider in Local Partnership

"All politics is local," the longtime U.S. Speaker of the House Thomas "Tip" O'Neill once famously declared. To that, I would add, "All healthcare is local." To solve the healthcare issues of today and the near future, I do not look to national government or to sweeping nationwide reform. This is not to say that national policy or nationwide initiatives do not add value. They do facilitate the local execution of certain models. Medicare's plan to incentivize providers to use e-prescribing is a good example of a national plan that will add value to local efforts.

But it is crucial that changes dictated at a national level not drive apart payers and providers. Any plans for national reform should avoid changes that could create more silos and negative incentives. Any policy created at 20,000 ft. must reflect awareness of the situation on the ground and the full effect changes might have.

Consider the problem of high hospital readmissions. If Medicare determines that hospital readmissions within 30 days are unacceptably high (and unacceptably costly), I do not think it solves the problem for Medicare to create a policy that refuses to pay for all readmissions. But I would think differently if the policy designated that a portion of the expected savings be returned to hospitals to invest in tools, technology, and staff members to manage patients better before and after discharge. That money could pay for better coordination with physicians at time of discharge or better patient education. Perhaps we would find that a $30 follow-up call could prevent a $5,000 readmission. Another scenario is for Medicare to pay a lower portion of its usual rate—perhaps just 70%—to hospitals with high readmission rates.

However, either scenario could cause hospitals to change aspects of admissions in ways that might increase the cost of admissions while reducing the chances of readmissions. We could find a setting where much more is spent up front to reduce spending on the back end. This is why I urge strong caution in developing any high-level policy that penalizes poor results without offering a solution for improving those results. Creating negative incentives and loopholes brings us back to the same kind of unaligned policies that we know do not work.

Regardless of what happens with national healthcare policy in the next few years, payers and providers will continue to interact. Whether we recreate unhealthy and counterproductive dynamics—or reject them—is up to us. But the unsustainable costs of the old strategies suggest they cannot continue. Alignment of payer and provider is the only viable option.

Outcomes-based reimbursement stands out as the truest means of aligning incentives. The greatest obstacle, perhaps, is that measuring outcomes is undeniably difficult. But it is not impossible. Achieving the alignment I have described is hard work. But alignment is the only process that will address the fundamental problems.

Constituencies with disparate interests, but a common goal, must work together. Analogies exist in many other endeavors. In the military, every branch of the service has its role, with its own methods and tactics. But when needed, the Army, Navy, Air Force, and Marines are able to work together in concert, as a team. If three branches succeed in a mission, but the fourth does not, the weak link can cause the whole strategy to break down. Similarly, in a team sport, every player has a role—be it defense, offense, shooter, and so on. How they come together is what makes them win. They win as a team, not as individuals.

I put forth these analogies because they are practical. We cannot solve our problems if we allow huge gaps or lack of engagement of any one constituent in the healthcare chain. When individuals confront illness, they require multiple interactions with different parts of the healthcare system. To achieve the best outcomes for patients, in the most cost-effective way, all of the constituents that interact with the patient must coordinate their efforts.

As we think beyond broad policies with a singular approach, our strategy must be to focus on the interdependencies that make good healthcare happen. We need to figure out, in any specific local area, the two, three, or four changes that will bring results. Implementing these changes likely will require that the payer, provider, employer, and patient all be aligned. We will learn from each other, one program at a time. The most effective programs will not be created with a cookie cutter. They will be created one by one.

This is a time of extraordinary opportunity. Technologies are available to help us unleash so many solutions, if we are willing to invest the time, effort, and resources that it takes to use them well. Everyone with a stake in healthcare has a role to play. It is time to roll up our sleeves and get to work—together.

ENDNOTES

1. The Commonwealth Fund, calculated from Organisation for Economic Co-operation and Development health data, 2006.

2. Ellen Nolte & C. Martin McKee, "Measuring the Health of Nations: Updating an Earlier Analysis," *Health Affairs,* January/February 2008 27 (1): 58–71.

3. 2008 Commonwealth Fund National Scorecard on U.S. Health System Performance.